# Wuthering Heights

## Adapted by Emma Rice

Based on the novel by Emily Brontë

*methuen* | drama

LONDON • NEW YORK • OXFORD • NEW DELHI • SYDNEY

METHUEN DRAMA
Bloomsbury Publishing Plc
50 Bedford Square, London, WC1B 3DP, UK
1385 Broadway, New York, NY 10018, USA
29 Earlsfort Terrace, Dublin 2, Ireland

BLOOMSBURY, METHUEN DRAMA and the Methuen
Drama logo are trademarks of Bloomsbury Publishing Plc

First published in Great Britain 2021

This edition published 2022

*Wuthering Heights* by Emily Brontë

Adapted for the stage by Emma Rice

Copyright © Emma Rice, 2021, 2022

Cover design: Rebecca Heselton

Cover image: Photography by Hugo Glendinning. Art direction
and design by National Theatre Graphic Design Studio.

A catalogue record for this book is available from the British Library.

A catalog record for this book is available from the Library of Congress.

ISBN: PB: 978-1-3503-3454-0
ePDF: 978-1-3503-3456-4
eBook: 978-1-3503-3455-7

Series: Modern Plays

Typeset by Mark Heslington Ltd, Scarborough, North Yorkshire

To find out more about our authors and books visit
www.bloomsbury.com and sign up for our newsletters.

# Wuthering Heights

*Wuthering Heights* was originally co-produced by the National Theatre, Wise Children, Bristol Old Vic and York Theatre Royal.

## CAST

| | |
|---|---|
| **Sam Archer** | Lockwood / Edgar Linton / The Moor |
| **Nandi Bhebhe** | The Leader of The Moor |
| **Mirabelle Gremaud** | The Moor |
| **TJ Holmes** | Robert / The Moor |
| **Ash Hunter** | Heathcliff |
| **Craig Johnson** | Mr Earnshaw / Dr Kenneth / The Moor |
| **Jordan Laviniere** | John / The Moor |
| **Lucy McCormick** | Catherine |
| **Kandaka Moore** | Zillah / The Moor |
| **Katy Owen** | Isabella Linton / Little Linton / The Moor |
| **Tama Phethean** | Hindley Earnshaw / Hareton Earnshaw / The Moor |
| **Witney White** | Frances Earnshaw / Young Cathy / The Moor |

The Moor is played by the ensemble. Like a Greek Chorus, whenever a performer is not playing a character they join The Moor to sing, dance and tell the story.

## THE BAND

**Sid Goldsmith**
**Nadine Lee**
**Renell Shaw**

With **TJ Holmes** and **Craig Johnson**

## CREATIVE TEAM

| | |
|---|---|
| Director | **Emma Rice** |
| Composer | **Ian Ross** |
| Set and Costume Designer | **Vicki Mortimer** |
| Sound and Video Designer | **Simon Baker** |
| Lighting Designer | **Jai Morjaria** |
| Movement Director and Choreography | **Etta Murfitt** |
| Puppetry Director | **John Leader** |
| | |
| Associate Director | **Laura Keefe** |
| Associate Choreography | **Nandi Bhebhe** |

| | |
|---|---|
| Puppetry Consultant | **Sarah Wright** |
| Fight Director | **Kev McCurdy** |
| Voice Coach | **Simon Money** |
| Lighting Programmer and Associate | **Victoria Brennan** |
| Music Supervisor | **Tom Knowles** |
| Costume Supervisor | **Anna Lewis** |
| Props Supervisor | **Lizzie Frankl for Propworks** |
| Associate Props Supervisor | **Fahmida Bakht for Propworks** |
| Wigs, Hair and Make Up Supervisor | **Dominique Hamilton** |
| Wigs, Hair and Make Up Associate | **Carly Roberts** |
| Prop Makers | **Propworks Workshop & Arianna Mengarelli** |
| | |
| The School for Wise Children Trainee Director | **John Leader** |
| The School for Wise Children Trainee Composer | **Mary Johnson** |

## PRODUCTION TEAM

| | |
|---|---|
| Production Manager | **Cath Bates** |
| Company Stage Manager | **Kate Foster** |
| Technical Stage Manager | **Aled Thomas** |
| Assistant Stage Manager | **Charlie Smalley** |
| Production Stage Manager | **Greg Shimmin** |
| Sound No 1 | **Charlie Simpson** |
| Sound No 2 | **Jimmy O'Shea** |
| Head of Wardrobe | **Amy Jeskins** |
| Wardrobe No 2 | **Emma Davidson** |
| | |
| Marketing | **Make A Noise** |
| PR | **Kate Morley PR** |
| Production & Rehearsal Photography | **Steve Tanner** |

## WISE CHILDREN TEAM

| | |
|---|---|
| Artistic Director | **Emma Rice** |
| Executive Producer | **Poppy Keeling** |

Wise Children is an Arts Council England National Portfolio Organisation. The original production of Wuthering Heights was additionally funded by an Arts Council National Lottery Project Grant, and by the Department for Culture, Media and Sport's Culture Recovery Fund.

## EMMA RICE

Emma Rice is the proud Artistic Director of her company Wise Children, and an internationally respected theatre-maker and director. Emma has adapted and directed all of Wise Children's productions: Angela Carter's *Wise Children*; Enid Blyton's *Malory Towers*, *Romantics Anonymous* and *Bagdad Cafe*.

As Artistic Director of Shakespeare's Globe (2016/18), she directed *Twelfth Night*, *A Midsummer Night's Dream* and *The Little Matchgirl (and Other Happier Tales)*.

For the previous twenty years, she worked for Kneehigh as an actor, director and Artistic Director and created critically acclaimed productions including *The Flying Lovers of Vitebsk*, *Tristan & Yseult*, *946: The Amazing Story of Adolphus Tips*, *The Wild Bride*, *The Red Shoes*, *The Wooden Frock*, *The Bacchae*, *Cymbeline* (in association with RSC), *A Matter of Life and Death* (in association with National Theatre), *Rapunzel* (in association with Battersea Arts Centre); *Brief Encounter* (in association with David Pugh and Dafydd Rogers Productions); *Don John* (in association with the RSC and Bristol Old Vic); *Wah! Wah! Girls* (in association with Sadler's Wells and Theatre Royal Stratford East for World Stages); and *Steptoe and Son*.

Emma received the Outstanding Contribution to British Theatre Award at the 2019 UK Theatre Awards. Acclaimed for her vision, wit, and warmth, she is one of the most dynamic and influential directors working in contemporary theatre today.


## WISE CHILDREN

Created and led by Emma Rice, Wise Children launched in April 2018 and is an Arts Council England National Portfolio Organisation. Based in the South West, we make ground-breaking work with exceptional artists, and tour across the world. In the dark days of 2020, we led the field in livestreaming, becoming the first UK company to broadcast a fully staged production, without social distancing, from a UK theatre after lockdown. Alongside our shows, we run a unique professional development programme, The School for Wise Children, training a new and more diverse generation of theatre practitioners.

# Wuthering Heights

**Prologue**

*The stage is a vast, hostile terrain inhabited by one solitary, bleak house.*

*Through the freezing rain and wind, we hear a voice from the auditorium.*

**Lockwood**   Hello! Hello! I say! Is anyone here?

*Knocking at the door of the house.*

Ho! Ho!

**Heathcliff** *opens the door of Wuthering Heights. He is stern and closed.*

Mr Heathcliff I presume?

**Heathcliff** *nods.*

Christmas greetings, dear neighbour!

**Heathcliff** *glowers.*

I am Mr Lockwood, your new tenant, sir. I wanted to call as soon as possible to express the hope that I have not inconvenienced you with my occupation of Thrushcross Grange!

*Still and fierce.*

**Heathcliff**   Thrushcross Grange is mine, sir, and I should not allow anyone to inconvenience me.

*He goes back indoors, shutting the door behind him.* **Lockwood** *is left awkward outside.*

*There is a huge gust of wind that throws him tumbling across the stage, through the mud and away from the house.*

*He gets back to the house and holds on tight. He knocks again.*

**Lockwood**   Hello! Ho, ho, ho! May I come in? It really is a little windy out here.

*The door opens and* **Heathcliff** *is again revealed. We see* **Young Cathy** *and* **Hareton** *unhappily behind him.*

Ah! At last! The warm Yorkshire family welcome I heard so much about! I could murder a cup of tea.

**Mr Lockwood** *enters the kitchen. He sits down but is immediately fixed upon by a dog. He goes to pat its head but it starts to growl at him.*

**Heathcliff**   You'd better leave the dog alone. She's not kept for a pet.

**Lockwood**   Ah! I understand.

*He winks and makes a face at the dog, which launches itself at him savagely.* **Lockwood** *throws the dog off and tries to keep it at bay.* **Young Cathy** *calls the dog away from* **Lockwood**, *who is visibly relieved.*

Thank you. I confess I didn't expect my entrance to be so exciting! I'd love that cuppa to calm my nerves.

**Young Cathy**   Were you asked?

**Lockwood**   What?

*She stands with a spoonful of the tea poised over the pot.*

**Young Cathy**   Were you asked to tea?

**Lockwood**   No. I was not asked, but perhaps you could ask me now?

*She flings the tea and spoon onto the floor and sits down with her back turned to* **Lockwood**. *The dog lunges at* **Lockwood** *again.*

Can someone please help me?

**Heathcliff**   She doesn't meddle with people who touch nothing.

**Lockwood**   I haven't touched anything! Please!

**Heathcliff** *gestures to* **Hareton** *who grabs the dog by the scruff and violently throws her away.*

Thank you, Sir. And thank you kind 'lad'.

**Heathcliff**   Why are you here?

**Lockwood**   I am come, Sir, out of festive politeness! However . . .

*He looks out of the window and sees snow coming down.*

I fear I might be weather-bound. Might you afford me a bed for the night?

**Heathcliff**   Why would you select a storm to ramble about in?

**Lockwood**   Perhaps your 'lad' could guide me home?

**Heathcliff**   No he could not.

**Lockwood**   Well, then, I must trust to my own finely tuned sense of direction and survival instincts. Farewell.

*He goes out onto the Moor where he is pelted with snow and battered by the winds. He crashes back into the Heights in distress.*

(*To* **Young Cathy**.) Please! Dear and amiable lady, please help me shelter from the storm.

**Heathcliff**   Amiable lady? Where is she? I see no amiable lady here.

**Lockwood**   Her! Mrs Heathcliff! Your wife.

**Heathcliff**   Mrs Heathcliff is dead.

**Lockwood** (*to* **Heathcliff**, *mortified*)   Oh! Forgive me, Sir.

**Heathcliff**   This Mrs Heathcliff is my daughter-in-law.

**Lockwood** (*to* **Hareton**)   Ah, I see now that you are the favoured possessor of this beneficent fairy.

**Hareton** *clenches his fist, with rage.*

**Heathcliff**   You are wrong, Sir. We neither of us 'own' your 'beneficent fairy'. Her mate is dead. I said she was my daughter-in-law: therefore, she must have married my son.

**Lockwood**   And this young man is . . .

**Heathcliff**   Not my son.

His name is Hareton Earnshaw and I'd counsel you to respect it.

**Lockwood**   I've shown no disrespect!

**Hareton** *moves to strike* **Lockwood**. **Lockwood** *puts up his hands in surrender.*

This visit was clearly a mistake. Sirs, Lady. Good night. And Oh! If you hear of me being discovered dead in a bog or a pit full of snow, your conscience won't whisper once that it is partly your fault, will it? Farewell.

*He opens the door, and the storm blows him to the ground.*

Oh! It is too wild. I need your help, kind Sir! I implore you to let me stay.

**Heathcliff**   If you stay you must share a bed with Hareton.

**Lockwood**   No. Please. I will happily sleep in this chair.

**Heathcliff**   I will not permit a stranger to range freely while I am off guard!

**Lockwood**   I am not a stranger, I am your tenant. I will not range and I will not touch. Please, show me some kindness!

*He is once again attacked and floored by the dog.* **Heathcliff** *and* **Hareton** *laugh out loud.*

**Heathcliff**   All. To bed. Mr Lockwood you may find a corner to rest in. But remember. Touch nothing.

**Heathcliff**, **Hareton** *and* **Young Cathy** *leave* **Lockwood**. *As the storm rages, he wanders the house until he finds a bed. He tucks himself up and finds a book by the window. In it is written:*

**Lockwood**   Catherine Earnshaw . . . Catherine Heathcliff . . . Catherine Linton. Catherine Earnshaw . . . Catherine Heathcliff . . . Catherine Heathcliff . . . Catherine Earnshaw.

*There is a gust of wind and the sound of a bough repeatedly tapping against the window.*

What is that?

*The branch, held by* **Catherine's Ghost***, keeps tapping on the window. Desperate and wild, she is searching for* **Heathcliff***.*

**Lockwood**    I must stop that infernal tapping!

**Lockwood** *forces his fist through the glass and stretches his arm out to stop the offending branch; instead of which, his fingers close on the fingers of* **Catherine's Ghost***.*

**Catherine's Ghost**    Let me in! Let me in!

**Lockwood**    Who are you?

**Catherine's Ghost**    Catherine Linton.

**Lockwood**    Linton? Why Linton? I had read Earnshaw and Heathcliff twenty times for Linton.

**Catherine's Ghost**    I'm come home! I lost my way on the Moor!

**Lockwood** *pulls her wrist down onto the broken pane. He rubs it to and fro until the blood runs down, soaking the bedclothes.*

Let me in!

**Lockwood**    How can I let you in when you hold on to me so tight? Let me go!

Release your grip if you want me to let you in!

*Her fingers relax and* **Lockwood** *pulls his hand to safety. He quickly blocks the window. Tricked,* **Catherine's Ghost** *moans with a doleful cry.*

**Catherine's Ghost**    Oh!

**Lockwood**    Begone Minx! I'll never let you in, not if you beg for twenty years.

**Catherine's Ghost**    It is twenty years. Twenty years. I've been a waif for twenty years!

*She scratches at the window so forcefully that* **Lockwood** *screams.*

**Lockwood**    Arghh.

**Heathcliff** *appears. He is shaking.*

**Heathcliff**    Who is here?

**Heathcliff** *stands at the door with a candle dripping over his fingers. The scream has startled him like an electric shock.*

**Lockwood**    It is I, sir. Lockwood. I'm sorry I disturbed you.

**Heathcliff**    Who showed you to this room? Who was it? Tell me!

**Lockwood**    Sir, it was I. In the absence of any hospitality from you or your companions, I found this room of my own accord.

**Lockwood** *rapidly starts to get dressed.*

And I wish, Sir, that I had not. This place swarms with ghosts and goblins! That wicked little soul! She told me she had been walking the earth for twenty years! A punishment for her living transgressions, I've no doubt!

**Heathcliff** *(savagely)*    How dare you! God! He is mad to speak to me so!

**Heathcliff** *strikes his forehead with rage.* **Lockwood** *is frozen in fear.*

Mr Lockwood, be gone.

**Lockwood**    I will! And do not fear a repetition of my visit. I'm now quite cured of trying to seek friendship!

**Heathcliff**    Go!

**Lockwood** *leaves.* **Heathcliff** *opens the window, and bursts into an uncontrollable passion of tears.*

Come in! Catherine, come in. Oh! My heart's darling! Do you hear me, Catherine? Come in!

**Lockwood** *stumbles onto the snowy Moor.*

*Figures begin to inhabit the space. They are wild and elemental. They are* **The Moor***. One steps forward and* **Lockwood** *is stopped in his tracks.*

**Lockwood**    Who are you?

**The Leader**    I am the Yorkshire Moor.

**The Moor**
    I am the Moor
    Ravaged by the stabbing rain,
    Wizened by the rascal sun,
    Tormented and mighty.
    I hold fast.

    I am the Moor
    Nothing here can shift me.
    Nothing here can change me.
    I stick to the earth and I stick to my story
    I am the Moor.

    I am the Moor.
    My story is wise as the crushing horizon
    Deep at the roots that anchor.
    My story is bigger than passing fancies
    Bigger than cruelty.
    My story turns the planet.
    And it's turning now.
    But I hold fast
    I am the Moor.

**The Leader**    What are you doing here?

**Lockwood**    I am trying to find my way home!

**The Leader**    Your home?

**Lockwood**    Yes. The warm and welcoming Thrushcross Grange.

*Looking back at The Heights.*

I can't understand why Mr Heathcliff would choose to live in this godforsaken place whilst renting The Grange to me? Is he not rich enough for comfort?

**The Leader**    Oh! He is rich! He has all the money in the world!

*We see **Heathcliff** looking for **Catherine** through the window.*

**Lockwood**    He had a son, it seems?

**The Leader**    Yes, he did. Linton Heathcliff. He is dead.

*We see **Linton Heathcliff**'s tomb stone.*

**Lockwood**    So the young lady, Cathy Heathcliff, is Linton's Heathcliff's widow?

*We see **Young Cathy** at the door of The Heights.*

**The Leader**    Yes. Young Cathy is Heathcliff's widow and daughter of Edgar Linton, also dead.

*We see **Edgar Linton**'s tombstone.*

**Lockwood**    So, she was born Cathy Linton? Then became Cathy Heathcliff?

**The Moor** *nods.*

So who was Catherine Earnshaw?

**Catherine's Ghost**    Let me in! Let me in!

**The Moor**    Shhh!

**Lockwood**    And who is Hareton Earnshaw?

*We see **Hareton** on the roof of The Heights.*

**The Leader**    He is the late Mrs Linton's nephew.

**Lockwood**    Mrs Linton?

**The Leader** Edgar Linton's wife. Young Cathy's Mother.

**Catherine's Ghost** *knocks on the window.*

**The Moor** Sshhh.

**Lockwood** (*trying to work it out*) Then Hareton is Young Cathy's cousin.

**The Moor** *nods.*

**The Leader** Yes.

**Lockwood** This is all too difficult. Far, far too difficult. How is anyone expected to follow this?

**The Moor** Try harder!

**Lockwood** Everyone's related, all the names sound the same and everyone is so very, very cross with me! I am cold and tired and I'm not ashamed to say, a little bit frightened. I am going home.

**The Leader** Stay. You are doing really well.

**Lockwood** I do not . . .

**The Moor** Stay!

**The Leader** Concentrate! No one said that this was going to be easy! Mrs Heathcliff's husband was also her cousin. She had one cousin on her mother's side.

**Lockwood** Hareton.

**The Moor** The other on the father's side.

**Lockwood** Linton? So Heathcliff must have married Edgar Linton's sister.

**The Leader** Isabella.

*We see* **Isabella***'s tombstone.*

**Lockwood** Dead?

**The Leader** All dead.

**Lockwood**   Enough! I'm going home.

*He goes to leave again, but* **Catherine's Ghost** *grabs his hand.*

**Catherine's Ghost**   How is he?

**Lockwood**   Who?

**Catherine's Ghost**   Heathcliff!

**Lockwood**   He is a rough, rude and rebellious fellow.

**The Leader**   Rough as a saw-edge, and hard as whinstone! The less you meddle with him the better.

**Lockwood**   And yet it is him that haunts me. Tell me, where did he come from?

**The Leader**   He was found by Mr Earnshaw.

**Mr Earnshaw** *appears.*

At the Liverpool docks.

## Part One

*The Moor transforms into the bustling Liverpool Dock. All of humanity is here. There is lots of man-made sound. Shouting. Ships' engines whirring. Music. Laughter.*

*In the centre of the hubbub a small dark boy is lost.* **Mr Earnshaw,** *a well-to-do gentleman, spots him. He looks around for an adult who might be responsible and on seeing none, kneels down to talk.*

**Mr Earnshaw**   Hello.

*The boy doesn't answer.*

There's nothing to be scared of. Who do you belong to? Eh? Where's your father? Your master?

*The boy lowers his brow and says nothing.*

Right, let's see if we can get you some help.

**Mr Earnshaw** *goes to take the boy's hand but he pulls away and runs into the crowd.*

As you like, boy. As you like.

**Mr Earnshaw** *goes back to his business but the boy reappears.*

Ah! You're back are you? What's your story eh?

*The boy starts to talk. The docks tell their stories. He is animated and expressive but speaks in a language no one can understand.* **Mr Earnshaw** *laughs with delight.*

Look at him! See how he shines. Black granite in the Liverpool rain. Words fall from him like chips from a sugar loaf. What have those young eyes seen, eh? A short lifetime of pain is my guess. And a short lifetime of loss.

(*To* **Heathcliff.**) Well, I'll never know where you've been, but I do know where you are going. You're coming with me, lad. Here's to long life and happiness. Can you say that, lad?

**All**   Long life and happiness!

**Mr Earnshaw**   I'm taking you home; home to Wuthering Heights where you can meet my children. Catherine and Hindley. Catherine and Hindley Earnshaw.

**Catherine** *and* **Hindley Earnshaw** *tumble on.* **Heathcliff** *is now hidden under* **Mr Earnshaw**'s *coat.*

**Mr Earnshaw**   I'm home!

**Catherine** *and* **Hindley**   Father, Father!

*They run to him and climb all over him with excitement. They check his pockets for presents but can't find anything.*

**Mr Earnshaw**   Now, my little juniper berries, you didn't think that your Father would come home empty handed did you?

**Catherine** *and* **Hindley**   What have you brought for us Father?

**Mr Earnshaw**   Close your eyes . . .

*They close their eyes . . .*

**Hindley**   Please let it be a fiddle, I want a fiddle.

**Catherine**   Please let it be a whip, I want a whip.

**Mr Earnshaw**   No fiddles or whips today my little Skylarks . . .

*He opens his coat, picks up* **Heathcliff** *and kisses him.*

Open your eyes!

*They open their eyes and look with horror.*

**Catherine** *and* **Hindley**   What is that?

**Mr Earnshaw**   'That', my Loves, is a new member of our family! I have called him Heathcliff.

**Catherine** *and* **Hindley**   Heathcliff?

**Mr Earnshaw**   Yes, Heathcliff. I cannot say why but I adore the boy. He is fine as a lapwing and rare as Cloudberry and I love him as my own. Welcome to our family, Heathcliff.

**Mr Earnshaw** *leaves the children together.* **Hindley** *cuffs him viciously across the face and laughs cruelly.*

**Hindley**    You are not family and never will be.

**Hindley** *exits and* **Catherine** *helps* **Heathcliff** *up. They take hands, lock eyes and the spell is cast.*

**Catherine**    Come on Heathcliff, I'll teach you the language of Yorkshire

**Heathcliff** *and* **Catherine** *run and play across the whole space. They are athletic and intimate, rough and fearless. They spot animals and plants.*

**Catherine**    Red grouse!

**Heathcliff**    Snipe!

**Catherine**    Bog Rosemary!

**Heathcliff**    Adder!

**Heathcliff** *and* **Catherine**    Bracken!

*They weave bracken and heather into crowns and wear them.*
**Catherine** *gazes at the sky while* **Heathcliff** *runs home, bumping into* **Hindley**. **Hindley** *snatches the crown from his head and puts it on his own.*

**Heathcliff**    Give it back.

**Hindley**    No.

**Heathcliff**    I said give it back.

**Hindley**    You go back. Go back to where you came from.

**Heathcliff**    This is my home. Give it back or I shall tell your father of the three thrashings you've given me this week.

**Hindley**    Make that four!

**Hindley** *cuffs him over the ears.* **Heathcliff** *lunges at* **Hindley**.

Off, dog!

**Hindley** *throws* **Heathcliff** *to the floor and pulls back his fist as if to hit* **Heathcliff**.

**Heathcliff** (*getting to his feet*)   Go on. Hit me, and then I'll tell your father how you boasted that you would turn me out of doors as soon as he died.

**Hindley** *thumps* **Heathcliff** *with all his might in the chest, and down he falls again.* **Heathcliff** *staggers up immediately, breathless. He raises his fists as if to fight more.*

**Catherine** *hears what is happening and tries to intervene.*

**Catherine**   Hindley. If you want the crown, you will have to take me on too. I have fight enough in me to take on an army.

**Heathcliff** *and* **Catherine** *scream like avenging angels. They are terrifying and as one.*

**Hindley**   Take it then, Gypsy! Take it, and be damned! Take it, and wheedle my father out of all he has. I hope one day he'll kick the brains out of your head!

*The three start to fight again.*

**Mr Earnshaw** *appears. He is furious with all of them.*

**Mr Earnshaw**   There'll be no more fighting. Not as long as I have breath in my body. Do you hear? I said do you hear me?

**Hindley**, **Catherine** *and* **Heathcliff**   Yes Father.

I love you all the same, whether you were born under this roof or under another sky altogether. I have enough love for all and so should you. Understood?

**Hindley**, **Catherine** *and* **Heathcliff**   Understood.

**Mr Earnshaw**   That, then, is that.

**The Leader**   But that, was not that.

*There is another scuffle, provoked by* **Hindley**.

**Mr Earnshaw**   Enough. Enough! Get out! Do you hear me? Get out of my house.

**Hindley**    But I'm your son.

**Mr Earnshaw**    You're no son of mine.

**Catherine**    Heathcliff. It is just you and me now!

*Their eyes lock. Waiting for an idea to land . . .*

**Heathcliff** *obliges and* **Catherine** *strikes him with her whip to make him run. He willingly plays along.* **Catherine** *goes to whip* **The Moor** *like a horse.*

**Mr Earnshaw**    Do not try your tricks with me, Catherine, for I will not bear your whipping and ordering.

**Catherine**    I am never so happy as when all are scolding me at once!

**Catherine** *sidles up to* **Mr Earnshaw**.

**Mr Earnshaw**    Catherine, thou art worse than thy brother. I rue that I ever reared thee!

**Catherine** *cries and laughs and runs back to* **Heathcliff**.

**The Leader**    Then came the hour that ended Mr Earnshaw's troubles on earth.

**Mr Earnshaw** *is seated by the fire-side. A high wind blusters round the house, and roars in the chimney. It is wild and stormy.*

**Mr Earnshaw**    Come Catherine. Heathcliff. Be still my wild ones. Be still.

**Catherine** *leans against her father's knee, and* **Heathcliff** *lies on the floor with his head in her lap.* **Mr Earnshaw** *strokes* **Catherine**'s *hair.*

Why canst thou not always be a good lass, Catherine?

*She turns her face up to his and laughs.*

**Catherine**    Why canst thou not always be a good man, father?

**Mr Earnshaw**   Come. Rest. Be at peace. Catherine, sing me that song I love.

*She kisses his hand and sings him to sleep. She sings 'The Bluebell' by Emily Brontë.*

**Catherine**
   The Bluebell is the sweetest flower
   That waves in summer air:
   Its blossoms have the mightiest power
   To soothe my spirit's care.

**Mr Earnshaw***'s fingers drop from* **Catherine***'s and his head sinks to his chest.* **Heathcliff** *gestures to* **Catherine** *to leave him sleeping.*

**Catherine**   I'm coming. But first, I shall bid him good-night.

**Catherine** *puts her arms round his neck and immediately discovers her loss.*

Oh, he's dead, Heathcliff! He's dead!

*They both give a heartbreaking cry. They sing.*

**Heathcliff** *and* **Catherine**
   The Bluebell cannot charm me now,
   The heath has lost its bloom;
   The violets in the glen below;
   They yield no sweet perfume.

**Lockwood**   God rest his soul, poor man.

**The Leader**   Poor man? He fanned the flames of hatred with his careless affections.

**Lockwood**   Oh.

**The Leader**   With his charity, he upset the natural order of things.

**Lockwood**   Ah.

**The Leader**   Speaking of the natural order of things.

**Hindley** *appears.*

**Hindley**   I'm home.

**Catherine**   Brother.

**Hindley**   Hello Catherine. Heathcliff.

**Heathcliff**   Hindley.

**Hindley**   Close your eyes.

*They close their eyes and* **Frances** *appears from inside his coat.*

Ta da! This is Frances, my wife. We are now the Master and Mistress of Wuthering Heights.

**Frances**   Oh Hindley! I love it! I totally love it! Look at the fire! Look at the pewter plates. Look at the children! Oh! I truly love it and love everything!

**The Leader**   What she was, and where she was from, Hindley never uttered.

**Lockwood**   One can only assume that she had neither money nor name, or else he would not have kept the marriage from his father.

**Frances**   Oh! I just love having a little sister! Catherine, come here and let me comb your hair. We shall be fine friends, won't we?

**Catherine**   Not if you comb my hair.

**Frances**   What can I do to help? I love to help. And I love you! Please what can I do? . . . oh!

*She bursts into tears and runs away. She curls up in a corner, rocking and wringing her hands.*

Oh! I am shaking. Catherine! Catherine, sister! Please, please come to my aid.

**Catherine** *looks at her with disdain.*

Hold me sister! Please, hold me.

**Catherine** *doesn't move.*

Please help, I fear I am dying.

**Catherine**   Dying? You are as likely to die as I am. Get up.

**Frances**   I cannot. See? I am a-quiver.

**Catherine**   Get up you silly woman.

**Frances**   I am not silly. I am unwell. I cannot mount the stairs without losing my breath and the least sudden noise sets my nerves a-jangle.

*She coughs.*

And I cough sometimes.

**Catherine** (*laughing*)   Heathcliff! Look at our new Mistress! She quivers and jangles and gasps like a new-born foal!

**Frances** *coughs.*

Oh and she coughs!

**Heathcliff** *and* **Catherine** *start to imitate her – coughing and shaking and jangling and gasping. It is a strange dance that is primal, frightening and funny.*

**Frances**   Husband! Please! Hindley, husband help me.

**Hindley** *enters and* **Catherine** *and* **Heathcliff** *quickly stop their dance.*

**Hindley**   What's the matter now, wife?

**Frances**   It was him.

**Hindley**   Who?

**Frances**   Heathcliff. He mocked me husband. He intimidated and scorned me.

**Hindley**   Did he indeed. Frances. You are the Mistress now and must behave like one.

**Frances** *gets up.*

Go and wash your face. I will deal with this.

**Frances** *scuttles off.* **Catherine** *glares at her.*

(*To* **Heathcliff**.) Get out.

**Catherine**    She was lying. It wasn't just Heathcliff.

**Hindley**    I said get out. You no longer live at Wuthering Heights.

**Catherine**    Hindley, no!

**Hindley**    You are no longer a guest, you are no longer a visitor and you are even less family.

**Catherine**    Please!

**Hindley**    From now on, you will sleep outside, like a dog. Your lessons will cease and you will work for your keep. And if . . . if . . . I see you set foot inside this house, or hear you so much as whisper to my wife or my sister you will be flogged like the beast you are. Do you understand me?

**Heathcliff** *glowers.*

I said, do you understand?

**Heathcliff**    I understand.

**Heathcliff** *leaves the house and, watched by* **Hindley**, **Frances** *and* **Catherine**, *stands outside on the Moor.*

**The Moor**
   Be careful what you seed.
   This black bog will close its fist
   around anything it can snag
   Cloudberry and Crowberry might
   dance on the surface
   But bullish bracken grips the bog in
   a headlock
   A scatter of yellow stars might
   seem to welcome hope
   But the adder slides beneath

The adder slides beneath
And what of the rage that is
planted?
The hate and jealousy that has
slipped into our watery beds?
Oh they grow alright.
They are coming along nicely, thank you,
In the warm wet earth
And they grow
Be careful what you seed.

**Lockwood**    But why did Heathcliff stay? If someone had said those terrible words to me I'd have bought a first-class ticket to town immediately.

**The Leader**    He stayed for Catherine. It was always, and only ever was, about Catherine.

**Catherine** *crosses to* **Heathcliff**.

**Heathcliff**    Why are you here?

**Catherine**    I missed you.

**Heathcliff**    You could be inside in the warm.

**Catherine**    I like it out here.

**Heathcliff**    You could be reading a book or embroidering an apron.

**Catherine**    I could.

*She goes to leave but* **Heathcliff** *grabs her and they tumble to the ground in a ball of giggles.*

Come on, let's run.

*They skip through the wind and the weather, ducking and diving.*

**Heathcliff**    What did you learn today?

**Catherine**    Nothing.

**Heathcliff**    I saw you through the window.

**Catherine**    I was learning to spell.

**Heathcliff**    To cast a spell?

**Catherine**    No! To spell my words in the way they tell me. But they are stupid. My words make sense to me so why should I care whether others can read them or not? If I ruled the world we could all spell as we wish, sing as we wished and dance as we wished.

*They dance a strange dance together.*

**Heathcliff**    Teach me how to spell.

**Catherine**    You have no need for writing.

**Heathcliff**    But I might. If I am to rule the world, I need to be able to play my enemies at their own game.

**Catherine**    Very well then. I will teach you. I will teach you everything, then we can rule the world together.

**The Moor**
    Ha!
    We shouldn't laugh, but this is
    something we don't often see.
    Look!
    Look how they slip through the
    earth's
    drag, find gravity in each
    other.
    Where does one end and the
    other begin?
    Oi!
    Watch it! I said watch it you two!
    Ha!
    We shouldn't laugh but this is something
    we don't often see.
    This is something rare and wild.
    Like juniper and bog
    rosemary.

*We hear the sound of a bird.*

**Heathcliff**   What is that?

**Catherine**   It's a bird.

**Heathcliff**   Where is it?

*They see a nest up high in a tree and climb it.*

**Catherine**   It's a Merlin.

**Heathcliff**   Where's its mother?

**Catherine**   It's been abandoned. I shall call it 'Heathcliff' after you!

**Heathcliff**   Do not name the poor creature after me. I am not to be pitied.

**Catherine**   Then I shall call him Nero.

**Heathcliff**   Nero?

**Catherine**   You really don't know anything, do you?

**Heathcliff**   How can I know things when I work like a slave and sleep with the animals?

**Catherine**   Nero was a great Roman Emperor. Adopted by his uncle, he was no ordinary man. An actor, a poet and a murderer, he cared deeply and cared not at all. He was ruthless and he was fierce. He was a magnificent tyrant.

**Heathcliff**   I like this Nero.

**Catherine**   So do I.

**The Moor**
  Careful! I said careful you two!
  This free fall is all very well but
  hold on tight to the curve of the
  earth or it will flick you off.
  Can you hear me?

**Heathcliff**   Let's go back. It's getting dark.

**Catherine**   No. I can see lights flickering at Thrushcross Grange. Let's go and see how the Lintons pass their Sunday evenings.

**Heathcliff**   I doubt they spend them shivering outside, while others sit laughing before the fire.

**Catherine**   Come on. We can fright them with our faces at their fancy fireside.

*The two run to Thrushcross Grange.*

**The Moor**
    You're pushing your luck, you two . . .
    Or is it one?
    Oi!
    You're pushing your luck! Wild Ones!
    No good can come from this feral joy.

**Catherine**   Look! Thrushcross Grange.

*They arrive at the house and look through the window. Inside, they see **Edgar** and **Isabella Linton**, who are fighting over a puppy. The interior is warm and colourful, all glass chandeliers and the warm glow of candlelight.*

**Isabella**   Edgar, I want to hold Constance. Give her to me.

**Edgar**   You are too rough, Isabella. She is my puppy and I want to hold her.

**Isabella**   Give Connie to me!

**Edgar**   I shan't.

**Isabella** *starts to cry.*

Oh don't. Please don't cry. Very well. Take her.

**Isabella**   I don't want her now.

**Edgar**   Then I don't want her either.

*The dog is left on the table whilst the two sulk and cry in opposite corners of the room.*

**Heathcliff**    The stupid powder puffs!

**Catherine** and **Heathcliff** *laugh and, on hearing them, the* **Lintons** *shoot like arrows to the door.*

**Isabella** and **Edgar**    Help! Robert! John! Come quickly! Outside, rascals! Scoundrels. Get them!

**Robert**    Skulker! Bristle! After them!

**Heathcliff** and **Catherine** *start to run away but* **Catherine** *falls just as a dog is let loose. The dog grasps her by the ankle and* **Heathcliff** *tries to prize it from her.*

**Catherine**    Run, Heathcliff, run! You cannot get him off me!

**Robert** and **John** *appear.*

**Robert** (*whistles*)    Skulker, stop.

*The dog stops and* **Robert** *kicks him away. He picks* **Catherine** *up, who is clearly in pain. He carries her indoors and* **Heathcliff** *follows.*

**Edgar**    What is it? Who is it?

**Robert**    Skulker has caught a little girl.

**John**    And there's a lad here with her who looks like a wrong 'un!

**Robert**    I bet robbers were going to put them through the window so they could open the doors to the gang! Then they could murder us in our beds!

**John**    Don't be silly. And don't you be afraid, children, it is but a girl and a boy!

**Edgar**    Frightful thing! Put him in the cellar.

**Isabella**    He's exactly like the son of the fortune-teller that stole my tame pheasant. Isn't he, Edgar?

**Edgar**    That's Miss Earnshaw from Wuthering Heights! Look how her foot bleeds!

**Robert**    Miss Earnshaw is it?

**John**    I've heard that her brother lets her grow up wild.

**Robert**    Then this one must be the acquisition the late Mr Earnshaw made . . . a fierce little Lascar.

**John**    Or an American.

**Robert**    Or a Spanish castaway.

**Heathcliff**    I am not a Lascar or American. I will tell you exactly what I am . . .

**Robert** (*cutting him off*)    That's enough, get out and stay out.

**Heathcliff** *is once more banished. He watches through the window at what happens inside.*

**Edgar**    You must stay here with us. I will look after you now.

**Catherine** *is sat on the sofa and* **Isabella** *gives her a cake.* **Edgar** *watches in awe and tends to her every desire.* **Catherine** *is delighted and thinks nothing of* **Heathcliff** *as she feeds her cake to the dogs.*

**Heathcliff** (*to* **The Moor**)    How full they are of stupid admiration! She is so immeasurably superior to them, to everybody on earth, is she not?

## Part Two

**Frances** *and* **Hindley**
God rest ye Merry Gentlemen
May nothing you dismay
Remember Christ our Saviour
Was born of Christmas Day
To save us all from Satan's pow'r
When we have gone astray.

**All**
Good tidings of comfort and joy,
comfort and joy,
Good tidings of comfort and joy.

God bless the ruler of this house
And send him long to reign
And many a Merry Christmas
May live to see again
Among his friends and kindred
That both live far and near
And God send them a happy new year
Happy new year
And God send them a happy new year.

**The Moor**
Five weeks is a blink for the planet,
But a lifetime for the lonely.
Five weeks is a hiccup for history,
But infinity for the lost.
Five weeks pass and Catherine comes
home
On a crisp, Christmas Eve.
Ankle cured,
Hair curled,
Feathered frock held aloft –
She floats.
She floats for fear of the earth.

She floats for fear of the truth.
She floats for fear of herself.

**Hindley**    Why, Catherine, Thrushcross Grange has suited you! Only five weeks away and you are quite a beauty! She looks like a lady now doesn't she, Frances?

**Frances**    She does! Look at her dress. Look at her red shoes.

**Catherine** *is revealed in a grand silk frock, white trousers, and burnished shoes. She checks herself in a hand mirror then looks for* **Heathcliff**.

**Catherine**    Is Heathcliff not here?

*She pulls off her gloves, and displays her fingers, wonderfully whitened with doing nothing.*

**Hindley**    Heathcliff, you may come and wish Miss Catherine welcome, like the other servants.

**Heathcliff** *appears and* **Catherine** *flies to embrace him, discarding the hand mirror as she goes. She kisses him over and over then draws back and bursts into laughter.*

**Catherine**    Why, how very cross you look! And how funny and grim! Well, Heathcliff, have you forgotten me?

**Hindley**    Shake hands, Heathcliff. Once is permitted.

**Heathcliff**    I shall not. I shall not stand here and be laughed at.

*He goes to leave, but* **Catherine** *stops him.*

**Catherine**    I did not mean to laugh at you, I just couldn't help myself. What are you sulky for? If you wash your face and brush your hair, it will all be put right! Heathcliff! Shake my hand at least.

**Heathcliff** *holds out his hand and* **Catherine** *recoils when she sees the filth.*

**Heathcliff**    You do not have to touch me. I am dirty, I like to be dirty, and I always will be dirty.

**Heathcliff** *leaves and it starts to snow.*

*As it snows, Christmas preparations begin and a tree is decorated by* **Catherine**, **Frances** *(now pregnant) and* **Hindley**. *They sing a carol.*

*It is Christmas Day.* **Heathcliff** *is working outside.*

**The Leader**    Heathcliff! It's Christmas Day and the Lintons are visiting! You must smarten up!

**Heathcliff** *doesn't move.*

Come on! Scrub up! If you don't change your ways, Catherine might be sorry she ever came home.

**Heathcliff**    Did she say that?

**The Leader**    She cried when you left.

**Heathcliff**    I had more reason to cry than she.

**The Leader**    Swallow your pride!

**Heathcliff** *sulks.*

(*Whispering.*) Edgar Linton looks like a fragile doll next to you. You could knock him down in a twinkling!

**Heathcliff**    If I knocked him down twenty times, it wouldn't make him less handsome. I wish I had straight hair and fair skin and a chance of being as rich as he is!

**The Leader**    Stop it! You are showing a poor spirit.

**The Moor** *washes his face and combs his hair and brushes down his clothes. They show him his image in* **Catherine**'s *mirror that they find in the earth.*

**Heathcliff**
    Cut through the dirt.
    What sleeps safe below?
    Slice through my clothes what's
    beneath?
    If I smooth down my hair what joys
    might be shown?

If I smile will they just see my
teeth?

**The Leader**    There! A prince in disguise!

Perhaps your father was Emperor, and your mother an
African queen! Come on Heathcliff! Dignity!

**Heathcliff**    Fuck dignity.

**The Leader**    Then fight!

**Heathcliff** *loses his frown, cracks a small smile and we see a
glimmer of hope. He sings.*

**Heathcliff**
If I play by the rules
What is lost from within?
Join in? Pretend? Will I melt?
If this snow drift of rage falls
sharp from my heart
What new griefs might bud and be
felt?

If she sees me afresh
It is worth every cut.
If she sees me anew
I am found.
If she'll dance with me,
Dream with me,
Sing with me,
Scream with me –

I will rip through my skin,
Tear up my soul,
Sever my limbs
Bury my past.
Just to rest.
Just to sleep.
Just to be . . .
With . . .

**Catherine**   They're here! Everybody quickly! The Lintons are here!

**The Lintons** *arrive, smothered in cloaks and furs.* **Catherine** *excitedly brings them into the house.*

**All**
　While shepherds watch
　Their flocks by night
　All seated on the ground
　The angel of the lord came down
　The angel of the lord came down
　And glory shone around
　And glory shone around
　And glory shone around.

*Rushing to join the party,* **Hindley** *and* **Heathcliff** *collide.*
*Irritated at seeing* **Heathcliff** *clean and cheerful,* **Hindley** *shoves*
**Heathcliff.**

**Hindley**   Stay away, Heathcliff.

**Heathcliff**   I will not!

**Hindley**   Begone I said!

*Seeing* **Heathcliff**'s *new look.*

What's this? A gentleman is it? Let me get hold of those thick black locks and see if I can pull them out of your wretched scalp!

**Edgar** (*peeping round the door*)   I wonder they don't make his head ache his locks are so heavy. Isn't he a wild thing!

*Enraged,* **Heathcliff** *seizes a jug of hot water and splashes it against* **Edgar**'s *face and neck;* **Edgar** *cries so loudly that* **Isabella** *and* **Catherine** *hurry to his aid.* **Hindley** *grabs* **Heathcliff** *and throws him outside.* **Edgar** *dabs at himself with a cloth and* **Isabella** *starts crying to go home.*

**Catherine** (*to* **Edgar**)   You should not have spoken to him! He was already in a bad temper and now he'll be flogged. I hate him to be flogged! I can't eat my dinner. And you, Edgar, have spoilt your visit. Why did you even speak to him?

*Whilst this conversation is happening,* **Hindley** *flogs* **Heathcliff** *brutally, outside in the snow.*

**Edgar**   I didn't speak to him. I promised myself that I wouldn't say one word to him, and I didn't. I just made a comment. One tiny comment.

**Catherine**   Don't cry! You're not killed.

**Isabella**   I want to go home!

**Catherine**   Shut up!! Has anybody touched you?

**Hindley** *comes in from the beating.*

**Hindley** (*red and breathless*)   Right! Time to feast! Exercise has warmed me nicely. Next time, Master Edgar, you should try taking the law into your own fists. It will give you an appetite!

*They all laugh.*

*Music! They start to eat a fine Christmas meal,* **Catherine** *is the perfect hostess, laughing and serving happily.*

**The Moor** *looks through the windows in disgust as* **Heathcliff** *lies bloody in the snow.*

**Dr Kenneth** *rushes past on his way to an emergency. He stops and checks* **Heathcliff**'*s pulse.*

**Dr Kenneth**   You'll live.

*Once the party is in full swing,* **Catherine** *slips away and joins* **Heathcliff** *in the snow. She collapses, tears rolling down her cheeks. They both give a heartbreaking cry.*

**Heathcliff** *and* **Catherine**
   The Bluebell cannot charm me now,
   The heath has lost its bloom;
   The violets in the glen below,
   They yield no sweet perfume.

**Catherine** *returns to the house, choosing comfort and status.* **The Moor** *taps* **Heathcliff** *on the shoulder.*

**The Leader**    What are you going to do now?

**Heathcliff**    Get my revenge on Hindley.

**The Leader**    Leave revenge to the Gods.

**Heathcliff**    No! The Gods won't have the satisfaction that I shall.

**The Moor** *tries to clean his wounds.*

Leave me! While I'm thinking of revenge I feel no pain.

*As* **Heathcliff** *exits, there is a scramble of activity between* **Frances** *and* **Dr Kenneth**. *An excited* **Maid** *comes running to* **The Moor**!

**Zillah**    I have news! Everyone, listen! I have wonderful news!

**The Leader**    What is it?

**Zillah**    A grand bairn!

**The Moor**    A bairn?

**Zillah**    Miss Frances! She has given birth to the finest lad that ever breathed!

**The Moor**    Hooray!

**Zillah**    But the doctor says she is not good.

**The Moor**    Oh.

**Zillah**    He says she'll be dead before spring.

**The Moor**    Dead?

**Zillah**    Yes dead! And in the meantime, I'm to nurse and feed it with sugar and milk. Perhaps he will be all mine when there is no Frances!

**The Moor**    Zillah!

**Zillah**    Sorry. But did I tell you what a beautiful bairn he is?

**Hindley** *and* **Dr Kenneth** *appear.*

**Dr Kenneth**    It's a blessing your wife has been spared long enough to leave you a son, as she surely won't last the winter. Don't fret about it too much, it can't be helped. And besides, you should have known better than to choose such a slender rush of a lass!

**Dr Kenneth** *exits.* **Hindley** *is clearly mad with grief.*

**The Leader**    What's his name?

**Hindley**    Whose name?

**The Leader**    The bonny bairn.

**Hindley**    We have called him Hareton.

**The Leader**    And how is baby Hareton?

**Hindley**    Nearly ready to run he is so strong and thriving.

**The Leader**    And Frances? The doctor said she's . . .

**Hindley**    Damn the doctor! Frances will be perfectly well by this time next week.

**Doctor** (*popping his head back in*)    I actually said that she's not . . .

**Hindley**    Begone!

**Frances** *runs to him, barefoot and in her nightclothes and jumps into his arms. He feels her burning brow and checks her tiny wrists.*

See! Her pulse is as slow as mine now, and her cheek as cool.

**Frances**    Yes! Yes husband! The fever is gone. I am feeling so much better. I might be able to get up tomorrow. Do you think I might get up tomorrow? Hindley?

**Hindley**    Frances? Frances!

*A fit of coughing takes her. She puts her arms around his neck, her face changes, and she dies.* **Zillah** *offers the baby to* **Hindley** *but he pushes it away.*

Take the brute away.

**Zillah**    Brute! He is a bonny beaming beauty!

**Hindley**   He killed my Frances. He killed my love. Take the bairn away and get me a drink.

*No one moves.*

I said get me a drink!

**Hindley** *descends into alcoholism.*

**The Moor**
   Life is a trickster.
   One trip and you're down.
   One slip and the fall begins.
   Hold on if you can,
   The planet is trying to shake you
   loose.
   Let go if you must and let the
   chaos take you.
   Let the chaos take you –
   If you must.

**Hindley** *collapses in a drunken stupor. Realising he is out cold,* **Heathcliff** *goes into Wuthering Heights to find* **Catherine**. *She is dressed prettily and obviously expecting someone else.*

**Heathcliff**   Are you going somewhere?

**Catherine**   No, it is raining.

**Heathcliff**   Then is someone coming here?

**Catherine**   Not that I know of. But you should be in the fields now, Heathcliff. It is an hour past dinnertime.

**Heathcliff**   Hindley is too drunk to notice. I'll not work any more today. I'll stay with you.

**Heathcliff** *lounges by the fire.*

**Catherine**   Oh. I almost forgot. Isabella and Edgar Linton talked of calling this afternoon. I hardly expect them; but they may come, and if they do, you run the risk of being scolded.

**Heathcliff**    Don't turn me out for those silly friends of yours! I'm almost at the point of complaining that . . .

**Catherine**    What are you at the point of complaining about, Heathcliff?

**Heathcliff**    That you spend more time with the Lintons than you do with me.

**Catherine**    Why should I spend time with you? You might be dumb, or a baby, for anything you say to amuse me!

**Heathcliff**    I hadn't realised that my company bored you.

**Catherine**    It's no company at all, when someone knows nothing and says nothing.

*There is a gentle knocking and* **Edgar** *enters, his face brilliant with delight at the unexpected summons he had received.* **Heathcliff** *leaves. They are day and night.*

**Edgar**    I'm not come too soon, am I? I understood from your invitation that . . .

**Catherine**    No. You are not too soon.

*Distracted by* **The Moor** *who is sweeping the floor.*

Psst. Take yourself and your brushes off.

**The Moor** *continues its work.*

I hate you to be fidgeting in my presence.

**The Moor** *works on. Enraged,* **Catherine** *grabs the broom and strikes* **The Moor** *with it spitefully.*

**The Moor** *screams.*

**Catherine** *goes to strike* **The Moor** *again.*

**The Moor** *screams.*

**Catherine**    I didn't touch you!

**The Moor** *screams.*

**Catherine** *slaps* **The Moor** *viciously.*

**Edgar**   Catherine!

**Catherine** (*to* **The Moor**)   Get out!

**Edgar**   Catherine, love!

**Hareton**, *who is being held by* **Zillah**, *starts to cry.* **The Moor** *stands firm. With a scream,* **Catherine** *grabs the child and shakes him.* **Edgar** *tries to restrain* **Catherine** *but she turns and strikes him full on the face. There is a shocked silence.*

**The Leader** (*to* **Edgar**)   Go! Now! It's a blessing that you have had a glimpse of her true disposition.

**The Moor** *leaves.* **Edgar**, *horrified, leaves with them.*

**Catherine**   Where are you going?

*She blocks the door. He swerves, and attempts to pass.*

You must not go!

**Edgar**   I must and shall!

**Catherine**   You shall not, Edgar Linton!

**Edgar**   How can I stay after you have struck me?

**Catherine**   You shall not leave me in a temper. If you do, I shall be miserable all night, and I won't be miserable for you!

**Edgar**   I make you miserable? You have made me afraid and ashamed of you. I'll not come here again!

**Catherine**   Edgar. Please! I did nothing deliberately.

**Edgar**   I have to go.

**Edgar** *doesn't falter.*

**Catherine** *drops down to her knees and starts to weep.* **Edgar** *leaves Wuthering Heights, encouraged by* **The Moor** *to get away. He gets as far as the gate when he can resist no longer.* **The Moor** *tries to hold him back but his desire is too great. He slips through their grip and races back to* **Catherine** *where they transition from friends to lovers. They get engaged.*

**The Moor**
    Life is a trickster.
    One trip and you're down.
    One slip and the fall begins.
    Hold on if you can,
    The planet is trying to shake you
    loose.
    Let go if you must.
    Let the chaos take you.
    Let the chaos take you –
    If you must.

**Edgar** *kisses* **Catherine** *goodbye and leaves.* **Heathcliff** *has dozed off by the fire. Unseen.*

**Catherine**   Where's Heathcliff?

**The Moor** *is silent.*

Edgar Linton has asked me to marry him, and I've given him an answer . . .

**The Moor** *is silent.*

I accepted him! Well? Say something! Was I wrong?

**The Leader**   Do you love him?

**Catherine**   Yes, I love him! I love the ground under his feet, and the air over his head, everything he touches and every word he says. I love all his looks, and all his actions, and him entirely and altogether!

**The Leader**   And why do you love him?

**Catherine**   Because he is handsome, and pleasant.

**The Leader**   Bad!

**Catherine**   Because he is young and cheerful?

**The Leader**   Bad, still.

**Catherine**   I love him because he loves me.

**The Leader**   And?

**Catherine**   Because he is rich, and I shall be the greatest woman of the neighbourhood.

**The Leader**   There it is!

**Catherine**   Am I wrong to marry him?

**The Leader**   Where is the obstacle?

**Catherine**   Here and here!

*She strikes one hand on her forehead, and the other on her breast.*

The obstacle is in my soul. And in my heart.

**Heathcliff** *wakes and starts to listen.*

I once dreamt I was in heaven, but it did not feel like home. My heart broke with weeping as I begged to come back to earth. The angels, angered, flung me out onto the Moor where I woke sobbing for joy. Heathcliff will never know how I love him. I love him not because he's handsome, but because he's more myself than I am. Whatever our souls are made of, his and mine are the same. Linton's is as different as a moonbeam from lightning, or frost from fire. I've no more business marrying Edgar Linton than I have to be in heaven – and if Hindley had not brought Heathcliff so low, I should never have even thought of it.

**The Leader**   Heathcliff?

**Catherine**   It would degrade me to marry Heathcliff now.

*There is a thunderclap.* **Heathcliff** *leaves. The planet turns.*

*The door slams as* **Heathcliff** *exits.*

What was that?

**The Leader**   It was Heathcliff. He was listening.

**Catherine**   He has not heard me, has he? No matter. Heathcliff does not know what it is to be in love!

**The Leader**  He knows as well as you! How will he bear to be separated from you?

**Catherine**  Who is to separate us, pray? I will not forsake Heathcliff. I will have both.

**The Moor**  You cannot have both. You have to choose!

**Catherine**  I have no choice. If Heathcliff and I married, we should be beggars. If I marry Linton I can help Heathcliff to rise, to place him out of my brother's grasp.

Everybody has a notion that there must be an existence beyond yourself. Heathcliff is mine. If all else perished, and he remained, I should still continue to be; and if all else remained, and he were gone, the universe would turn into a mighty stranger. My love for Linton is like foliage in the woods: time will change it. My love for Heathcliff resembles the eternal rocks beneath. I am Heathcliff! He's always, always in my mind: not as a pleasure, but as my own being.

*There is a clap of thunder and the heavens open.*

Heathcliff! Heathcliff!

**Catherine** *runs out in the rain to find him. She calls and runs across the moors but he is gone.*

**Heathcliff**
  I smudge you.
  I smudge you as you
  Wash your faces morn and night,
  Douse your wrists with smells of
  fruit and petals,
  Dance, using sorrows as stepping
  stones
  And imagine that your bird light
  hearts beat with love.
  I smudge your happy faces.
  I douse your sweet smelling necks
  with filthy rain
  I force you to your knees in the
  mud.

I push your head down to the soil
and
I scream 'dig'.
I laugh as you push your brittle
bird hands into the earth and sing
as your porcelain fingers hit the
black marsh.
Siltstone, sandstone, millstone,
gritstone.
I call on you.
I call on you to drag them down.
Spare them no anguish.
I feel nothing.
They can do that for me.
Dig!
Into the dirt
Into the rage
Into the truth

And get stuck there, as I have been
stuck for hundreds of years

I smudge you.

*He leaves.*

**Catherine**    Heathcliff! Heathcliff! Heathcliff!

**Catherine** *curses.*

**Catherine**
Look up!
The stars hang high tonight,
Look up!
The stars hang high tonight.
Discarded skin on blackened sky.

I am the earth.
I am the earth.
I am the earth.
I am the earth.

I cast a shadow on your twinkle.
I cast a shadow on you all.

I am the earth.
I am the cry.
I am the blood.
I am the sky.

I fuck the world.
I shout my rage.
I curse the word upon the page.

I am the earth, I won't lose my
grip,
I choose the dark, my sex I strip
Fuck you all, fuck the stars,
You split my head, I wear the
scars.

I won't let go.
I won't let go.
I am the earth.
I am the blood.
I am the world.
I am the girl.
I am the star.
I am the blood.
I am the earth.

## Part Three

**Catherine** *is dressed as a bride.* **Edgar** *appears as a groom and almost faints at the sight of* **Catherine**'s *beauty. After the wedding,* **Edgar** *and* **Catherine** *sit sedately and quietly, at peace in their new life.*

**The Leader**
Home can come in many forms
Person, place or beast
It soothes the soul and strokes the brow
Gives rest, for now, at least.

**Edgar** *and* **Catherine**
Time can cool the heat of youth
Calm replaces rage
Silence now a scream drowns out.
Peace and war assuage.

**The Leader**   Yes. She married Edgar Linton. Yes. She scraped the earth from beneath her nails and married Edgar.

**Isabella** (*to* **The Moor**)   What has happened to Heathcliff?

**The Leader**   Who knows what happened in those lost years.

**Isabella**   Perhaps he escaped to America to make his fortune? Or turned to crime on the English highways!

**The Leader**   The only thing that is certain is that Heathcliff returned, three years to the day, as fine a gentleman as you will ever see.

**Heathcliff** *appears. He is athletic and well dressed.* **Isabella** *almost faints at the sight of* **Heathcliff**'s *beauty.*

**Heathcliff**
I will rip through my skin,
Tear up my soul,
Sever my limbs

And bury my past.
Just to rest.
Just to sleep.
Just to be . . .
With . . .

**Catherine** *on hearing his voice, jumps with joy.*

**Catherine**    Oh, Edgar, Edgar! Oh, Edgar darling!
Heathcliff's come back!

**Edgar**    The gypsy? The plough boy?

**Catherine**    You must not call him by those names. He is a
gentleman now.

**Edgar**    There is no need to be frantic!

**Catherine**    I know you don't like him, but, for my sake, you
must be friends now.

Shall I tell him to come up?

**Edgar**    Here? Heathcliff come into the parlour?

**Catherine**    Where else?

**Catherine** *and* **Edgar** *glare at each other.*

Set two tables then, dear. One for you and Miss Isabella,
being gentry; the other for Heathcliff and myself, being of
the lower orders.

**Edgar**    Stop it Catherine.

**Catherine**    I'll run down and get him!

**Edgar** *stops her.*

**Edgar**    I will invite him up. Catherine, try to be glad,
without being absurd. The whole household need not
witness the sight of you welcoming a runaway servant as a
brother.

*He calls out of the door.*

Mr Heathcliff. Welcome, sir.

**Heathcliff** *enters and after a moment of silence,* **Catherine** *seizes* **Heathcliff** *and* **Edgar** *and forces them to hold hands. She laughs like one beside herself and flings her arms around* **Heathcliff**'s *neck.* **Edgar** *sits down.*

**Catherine**   I shall think it a dream tomorrow! I shall not be able to believe that I have seen, and touched, and spoken to you once more. And yet, cruel Heathcliff! You don't deserve this welcome. To be absent and silent for three years, and never to think of me!

**Heathcliff**   I have thought of you more than you have thought of me. I heard of your marriage, Cathy and, while waiting to be invited in, I hatched a plan.

**Catherine**   A plan?

**Heathcliff**   My plan was to have one last glimpse of you, settle my score with Hindley then kill myself to put an end to this life of misery.

**Catherine**   No!

**Heathcliff**   Indeed! Your welcome has put these ideas out of my mind for now.

**Catherine**   Good! But Heathcliff, where have you been?

**Edgar**   Catherine, unless we are to have cold tea, please come to the table. Isabella! We have a guest.

**Isabella** *enters and giggles.*

Tea, Mr Heathcliff? You will need one before your long walk back to your lodgings.

**Isabella**   And where are you lodging tonight, Sir? I'm sure we have room enough . . .

**Edgar**   Isabella! No!

**Heathcliff**   Do not worry, Sir. I am staying at Wuthering Heights. Mr Earnshaw invited me, when I called on him this morning.

*We cut to a scene in Wuthering Heights. A group of drunken men are gambling.* **Hindley** *loses and* **Heathcliff** *lends him money.*

**Hindley**    Come back tonight and I will repay you!

**Heathcliff**    Of course you will. Of course.

**Catherine**    I have never been so content in my whole life.

**The Leader** (*to* **Catherine**)    Catherine! Do you not fear the consequences! For you? For Edgar? For Heathcliff?

**Catherine**    I fear not for Heathcliff, his strength will keep him from danger. As for Edgar, I'll make my peace with him instantly.

**The Moor**    Will he want your peace?

**Catherine**    I have such faith in Edgar's love, that I believe I might kill him, and he would forgive me. Goodnight! I'm an angel!

**Catherine** *goes and cuddles up to* **Edgar** *while* **Heathcliff** *returns to Thrushcross Grange.* **Isabella** *welcomes him.*

**Isabella**    How was your journey, Mr Heathcliff? Can I take your coat, sir?

**Catherine** *rushes in and jumps on* **Heathcliff** *with joy.*

**Catherine**    Heathcliff! I have so much to tell you!

*They walk together with* **Isabella** *trying to join in.*

**Isabella**    Oh yes, me too!

**Catherine**    Isabella! Go away! Leave me alone with Heathcliff.

**Edgar**    Catherine! Could you come here a moment?

**Catherine** *runs to* **Edgar** *and showers him with kisses.*

**Isabella**    If you are without company Mr Heathcliff, I could walk with you?

**Catherine** *runs back and sees* **Isabella** *with* **Heathcliff.**

**Catherine**   Run along little girl. Mr Heathcliff does not want to waste his time with a child.

**Heathcliff**   Excuse me ladies, I have an appointment to play cards.

**Heathcliff** *says goodbye as* **Isabella** *fumes and* **Edgar** *looks out of the window, clearly worried.*

**Isabella**   You are too harsh, Catherine Linton. Too harsh.

**Catherine**   When?

**Isabella**   Just now, sister.

**Catherine**   That's your notion of harshness! Your company was superfluous. We didn't care whether you were with us or not.

**Isabella**   You pushed me away, because you knew I wanted to be there!

**Catherine**   Are you mad? I'll repeat our conversation, word for word if you like.

**Isabella**   I didn't want the conversation, I wanted to be with . . .

**Catherine**   With?

**Isabella**   With him! You are a dog in the manger, Catherine, and desire no one to be loved but yourself! I love him more than you ever loved Edgar, and he might love me, if you would let him.

**Catherine**   I wouldn't be you for a kingdom, then! I'd as soon put a canary onto the Moor on a winter's day, than recommend you bestow your heart on Heathcliff! And don't imagine that he conceals depths of affection beneath that stern exterior!

He's a fierce, pitiless, wolfish man. He'd crush you like a sparrow's egg, Isabella.

**Isabella**    Why would you want to tell me that there is no happiness in the world?

**Catherine**    Because there is no happiness. Heathcliff will never love you, Isabella – but he is quite capable of marrying you for your fortune.

**Isabella**    For shame, Catherine! For shame!

**Catherine**    You're coming with me.

**Heathcliff** *is back at Wuthering Heights. He gives money to the drunk* **Hindley** *who is losing it at poker.*

**Catherine** *and* **Isabella** *glare.* **Heathcliff** *appears.*

**Catherine**    Heathcliff! We need you to resolve our conflict!

**Heathcliff**    Conflict?

**Catherine**    Here is somebody that dotes on you more than I do! My poor little sister-in-law is breaking her heart with the mere contemplation of your physical and moral beauty.

**Isabella**, *mortified, tries to run out but* **Catherine** *catches her.*

We have been quarreling like cats about you, Heathcliff!

**Isabella**    Mr Heathcliff, please be kind enough to bid this friend of yours release me: she forgets that you and I are not intimate acquaintances and what amuses her is painful to me beyond expression.

**Heathcliff**    You are wrong, Catherine. She only wants to be out of my society at the moment.

**Catherine** *smiles.* **Heathcliff** *stares at* **Isabella**. **Isabella** *digs her nails into* **Catherine**'s *arm and tries to break free.*

**Catherine**    There's a tigress! How foolish to reveal those talons to him! Look, Heathcliff! You must protect your eyes.

**Isabella** *runs out in distress.*

**Heathcliff**    I'd wrench her nails off her fingers, if they ever menaced me.

*They smile at each other.*

You were not speaking the truth, were you?

**Catherine**    I was! But don't think about her anymore. I like her too well to let you devour her up.

**Heathcliff**    And I like her too ill to attempt it.

*They smile at each other.*

She's her brother's heir, is she not?

**Catherine**    Don't even think about it! Half a dozen nephews will put a stop to any inheritance she might be owed!

**Heathcliff**    Thank you for telling me your sister-in-law's secret: I swear I'll make the most of it.

*They smile at each other.*

You have treated me infernally, Catherine. If you think I'll go unrevenged, you are deceived!

**Catherine**    Revenge? On me?

**Heathcliff**    Not on you. Never on you. You are welcome to torture me to death for your amusement. Only allow me to amuse myself a little in the same style.

**Edgar** *appears who has been listening at the door.*

**Edgar**    This is insufferable! Catherine, it is disgraceful that you should force this beast on me!

**Catherine**    Have you been listening at the door, Edgar?

**Heathcliff** *laughs.*

**Edgar**    I have so far borne you, sir, not because I was ignorant of your miserable, degraded character, but because Catherine wished to keep your acquaintance. I have been foolish, however, and I therefore deny you further admission into this house and require your instant departure.

**Heathcliff** *measures the height and breadth of the speaker with an eye full of derision.*

**Heathcliff**    Catherine, this lamb of yours is in danger of splitting his skull against my knuckles.

**Edgar**, *fearful, goes to leave but* **Catherine** *blocks his way.*

**Catherine**    If you do not have the courage to attack him, Edgar, make an apology. No? Nothing? Then allow yourself to be beaten!

**Edgar** *starts a nervous trembling. Anguish and humiliation overcome him completely. He sits, and covers his face.*

Get up! Heathcliff would as likely hit you as a king would march his army against a battalion of mice. Get up!

**Heathcliff**    Look at the milk-blooded coward. Look at the slavering, shivering thing you preferred to me!

**Heathcliff** *kicks* **Edgar**'s *chair.* **Edgar** *springs up and punches* **Heathcliff** *on the throat.* **Heathcliff** *is winded and* **Edgar** *leaves.*

**Catherine** (*to* **Heathcliff**)    There! Are you happy? Now you can never come here again! Get away from me! Leave!

He'll be back with half a-dozen men. Go!

**Heathcliff**    I'll crush his ribs like a rotten hazelnut before I leave!

**Edgar** *returns with help. They are armed.* **Heathcliff** *escapes just as they enter.*

**Catherine** (*to* **The Moor**)    A thousand smiths' hammers are beating in my head! This uproar is Isabella's fault. What possessed Edgar to listen in to us? And Heathcliff's talk was outrageous. I have to get out.

**Catherine** *goes to leave.*

**Edgar**    Remain where you are, Catherine. I have not come to wrangle or be reconciled with you. I simply wish to learn whether you intend to continue your intimacy with . . .

**Catherine**   For fuck's sake Edgar! 'Continue my intimacy'? Your veins are full of ice-water! But mine, mine are boiling, and the sight of your chilliness makes them dance.

**Edgar**   If you want to get rid of me, answer my question. Will you give up Heathcliff or will you give up me? I require to know which you choose.

**Catherine**   I require to be let alone! I demand it! Don't you see I can scarcely stand? Leave me! Get out!

**Catherine** *dashes her head against the arm of the sofa, and grinds her teeth. She stretches herself out stiff, and turns up her eyes, while her cheeks, blanched and livid, assume the aspect of death.*

**Edgar**   Help! Someone help her!

**The Leader**   Nothing is the matter with her.

**Edgar**   She has blood on her lips!

**The Leader**   She is pretending. Go away and stay away. We will deal with her dissembling.

**Catherine** *springs back to life, wild. She locks herself in her room and starts wrecking it.*

**The Moor**
  Stop it!
  Slow down or you'll break
  something!
  Cool down or you'll break yourself!
  You've pretended so long, your lies
  have become truths.
  Stop it!
  We said stop it you mad creature.

**Catherine**   I have to get out.

*She runs to the window and tries to get out.* **The Moor** *stops her.*

**The Moor**
  Stop it!
  Slow down or you'll hurt yourself!

Get down or you'll hurt someone else!
You can't tell wrong from right
Stop it!
We said stop it you monster.

*We see* **Edgar** *reading in his study, trying to block out the commotion.*

*We see* **Heathcliff** *whispering in* **Isabella**'s *ear.*

**Catherine** *opens the window.*

**Catherine**    Look! My room! I can see my room at Wuthering Heights! It's the one with the candle in it, and the trees swaying before it. It's a rough journey home and we must pass the church! We've often braved its ghosts and dared each other to stand among the graves and ask them to come and get us if they dared.

But, Heathcliff, if I dare you now, will you venture? I'll not lie there by myself. They may bury me twelve feet deep, and throw the church down over me, but I won't rest till you are with me!

**Edgar** *enters.*

**Edgar**    Catherine! Oh God! They told me . . . Oh God.

*He shuts the window and holds* **Catherine** *close and cradles her.*

**Catherine**    Ah! You are finally come, are you? Come to keep me from my grave, Edgar Linton? My grave is in the open air. I will not be trapped under the chapel roof. Trapped with the Lintons. It is up to you whether you go to them or come to me when you are dead!

**Edgar**    Catherine, what are you saying? Am I nothing to you any more? Do you love that wretch Heathcliff?

**Catherine**    You mention that name again and I will end the matter instantly with a spring from the window! I don't want you, Edgar. I'm past wanting you. Return to your books. I'm glad you possess a consolation, for all you had in me is gone.

*We see* **Heathcliff** *and* **Isabella** *leave together, as lovers.*

**The Leader**    Edgar Linton. Edgar Linton!

**Edgar**    What is the matter?

**The Leader**    She's gone! Isabella has gone.

**Edgar**    What do you mean?

**The Leader**    With Heathcliff. Heathcliff has taken Isabella!

**Edgar**    By force?

**The Leader**    Not by force.

**Edgar**    She'll be back.

**The Leader**    Not as Miss Linton. She has married him! She has married Heathcliff.

**Edgar**    Then trouble me no more with her. Hereafter she is only my sister in name, not because I disown her, but because she has disowned me.

**Edgar** *returns to nurse* **Catherine**.

**Isabella** *walks forwards, lost and alone. She addresses the audience.*

**Isabella**    Hello.

I have no other friend to talk to, so might I trouble you? Would that be ok? Thank you.

I beseech you to explain, if you can, what I have married. Is Mr Heathcliff a man? If so, is he mad? And if not, is he a devil?

I now live at Wuthering Heights and it is a far cry from Thrushcross Grange! When I first arrived, Heathcliff locked the door behind him and left me alone.

**Hareton** *appears. A ruffian child with a look of* **Catherine**.

**Isabella**    How do you do? You must be Hareton? You are almost my nephew if I am not mistaken. Shall we be friends?

**Hindley** *appears. He is a wreck. Gaunt and frightening.*

**Hindley**    Get out, Hareton! Who are you? What's your business here?

**Isabella**    My name was Isabella Linton. You've seen me before, sir. One Christmas here, at the Heights.

I'm lately married to Mr Heathcliff, and he has brought me here, I hope, with your permission.

**Hindley** *drinks.*

Might I call the maid, and be conducted to a bedroom? I'm tired with my journey, and I want to go to bed. Where is the maid-servant?

**Hindley**    There is no maid servant. You must wait on yourself!

**Isabella**    Where must I sleep, then?

**Hindley**    Heathcliff's chamber as you are his wife.

*He gestures to a door.* **Isabella** *tries the door but it is locked.* **Hindley** *laughs.*

When you and he do go to bed, be so good as to turn your lock. Draw your bolt as well and don't forget it!

**Isabella**    But why, Mr Earnshaw?

**Hindley** *takes out a pistol.*

**Hindley**    This is a great tempter for a desperate man. Every night I try his door. If once I find it open, he's done for. And when the time comes, all the angels in heaven cannot save him!

**Isabella** *takes the pistol.*

**Isabella**    How powerful I should be if I possessed such an instrument . . .

**Hindley** *snatches the pistol back.*

What has Heathcliff done to you to warrant this hatred? Wouldn't it be wiser to ask him to leave?

**Hindley**  He cannot leave! Must I lose all? Is my son, Hareton, to be a beggar? I am Heathcliff's slave, but he will not be the victor. I will win back my house, steal his gold and drink his blood. Hell can have his soul!

**Hindley** *leaves.*

**Isabella**  Please. My room is locked and I must sleep. Please give me a key or show me another chamber.

**Heathcliff** *appears.*

**Heathcliff**  What are you doing?

**Isabella**  I could not get into our room as you alone have the key.

**Heathcliff**  It is not, nor ever shall be, our room!

*He violently pushes her into the dark.* **The Moor** *covers what is happening. We know this is sex. We know this is without love. But we do not see.* **Heathcliff** *leaves her.*

**Isabella** (*to the audience*)  Please don't tell Edgar. Please. I am so ashamed.

Remember my name please. I am Isabella Linton. No. I forgot. I am Isabella Heathcliff. I don't want to disappear.

**Edgar,** *seeing that* **Catherine** *is failing, runs to get the doctor.*

**Edgar**  Dr Kenneth! Please! Quickly doctor, quickly!

*We see* **Dr Kenneth** *crossing the Moor to help and* **Edgar** *running out of Thrushcross Grange to find him.*

**The Leader**  Heathcliff! Heathcliff

**Heathcliff**  What is it?

**The Leader**  It is Catherine.

**Heathcliff**  Catherine?

**The Leader**  Go to her. Quickly. There is no time. Run.

**Heathcliff** *runs to Thrushcross Grange.*

**The Moor**
Life is a trickster.
One trip and you're down.
One slip and the fall begins.
Hold on if you can,
The planet is trying to shake you
loose.
Let go if you must and let the
chaos take you.
Let the chaos take you –
If you must.

*He does not find the right room directly, but in a stride or two he is at her side, and grasps her in his arms.*

**Heathcliff**   Oh, Catherine! Oh, my life! How can I bear it?

**Catherine**   What? How can you bear it? You and Edgar have broken my heart, Heathcliff! And you both come to bewail the deed as if you were the people to be pitied! I shall not pity you. You have killed me and thrived upon it. Look how strong you are! How many years do you mean to live after I am gone?

**Heathcliff** *kneels and embraces her. He attempts to rise, but she seizes his hair, and keeps him down.*

I wish I could hold you till we are both dead! I shouldn't care if you suffer.

Why shouldn't you suffer as I do! Will you forget me? Will you be happy when I am in the earth?

**Heathcliff**   Don't torture me til I'm as mad as you are! Why would you talk to me like this when you are dying? These words will be seared into my memory, and will eat eternally deeper after you have left me. You know that I could as soon forget you as my existence! Is it not enough for your infernal selfishness, that when you are at peace I shall writhe in the torments of hell?

**Catherine**   I shall not be at peace. I wish only for us to never be parted. Come here and kneel again! You never harmed me in your life. Nay, if you nurse your anger, that will be worse for you to remember than my harsh words! Won't you come here again? Please . . .

**Heathcliff** *returns to her chair but he cannot bear it and turns his back to* **Catherine**.

You leave me? When I beg? You are not my Heathcliff. I shall take mine with me: he's in my soul.

*There is a rush of wind from the Moor.*

I'm tired of being enclosed here. I want to escape into that glorious world, and to be always there: not seeing it dimly through tears, and yearning for it through the walls of an aching heart: but really with it, and in it. Very soon I shall be beyond and above you all. Do you hear me? And yet I wonder why you won't be near me now? Do come to me, Heathcliff.

**Catherine** *rises.* **Heathcliff** *turns to her and then* **Catherine** *makes a spring and* **Heathcliff** *catches her. They are locked in an embrace from which it looks like* **Catherine** *will never be released alive.*

**Heathcliff**   You loved me, Catherine. You loved me. What right had you to leave me?

What right had you to break us in two? Nothing that God or Satan could inflict would have parted us. It was you. You, of your own will, did it. And for what? For the poor fancy you felt for Edgar? I have not broken your heart, you have broken it; and in breaking it, you have broken mine. Why did you betray your own heart, Catherine?

**Catherine**   If I've done wrong, I'm dying for it.

**Heathcliff**   I have not one word of comfort for you. You have killed yourself.

**Catherine** Enough! You left me too, remember? But I forgive you. Now you must forgive me! I am dying and you will live.

**Heathcliff** Live? What kind of living will it be when you . . . When you . . . oh, God! How can I live with your soul in the grave? Answer me that, Catherine?

**Edgar** *is seen coming through the gate. He is heading to* **Catherine**.

**The Leader** He returns! Edgar Linton returns.

**Heathcliff** I must go, Catherine.

**Catherine** You must not go!

*She holds him as firmly as her strength allows.*

You shall not, I forbid you.

**Heathcliff** For one hour only.

**Catherine** Not for one minute.

**The Leader** Edgar Linton returns!

**Heathcliff** I must.

**Catherine** *clings fast, a mad resolution in her face.*

**Catherine** No! Please don't go. It is the last time! I know it. Edgar will not hurt us. Heathcliff, I die! I die!

**Heathcliff** Hush, hush, my darling Catherine! I'll stay. If he shoots me, I'll die with you on my lips.

*They kiss.*

**The Leader** No! Heathcliff! Do not listen to her ravings! She does not know what she says. Get out! She cannot help herself so you must help her.

**Heathcliff** (*still holding* **Catherine** *in his arms*) Help her? By leaving? You know nothing, you understand nothing.

**Catherine**'s *arm falls and her head drops.*

**The Moor**    Oh!

**Heathcliff**    Catherine!

**Edgar** *enters.*

**Edgar**    Heathcliff!

**Heathcliff** *passes the lifeless-looking form of* **Catherine** *into* **Edgar**'s *arms.*

**Heathcliff**    Help her first, then you shall speak to me.

**Edgar** *takes* **Catherine** *and brings her back to consciousness.* **Heathcliff** *watches until he sees she lives, then joins* **The Moor** *outside.*

**The Leader**
   I am the Moor
   Ravaged by the stabbing rain,
   Wizened by the rascal sun,
   Tormented and mighty.
   I hold fast.

*We see* **Isabella** *escape from Wuthering Heights and run for her life. She is clearly pregnant.*

**The Moor**
   I am the Moor
   Nothing here can shift me
   Nothing here can change me.
   I stick to the earth
   And I stick to my story
   I am the Moor.

*We see* **Hindley** *drink himself to death. Hareton tries to bring his father back to life but is left. Alone.*

**The Moor**
   My story turns the planet.
   And it's turning now.
   But I hold fast
   I am the Moor.

**Dr Kenneth** *arrives and there is a commotion around* **Catherine** *and then a baby's cry.*

**Edgar**   Catherine! Catherine! No!

*We see* **Catherine** *is dead.* **Zillah** *offers the baby to* **Edgar** *but he cannot bear to take the child.* **Dr Kenneth** *prepares* **Catherine***'s body and* **Edgar** *lies down beside his wife.*

**The Leader**   She's dead.

**Heathcliff**   I know.

**The Leader**   May she wake at peace in another world.

**Heathcliff**   May she wake in torment! Catherine Earnshaw, haunt me!

Be with me always, take any form, drive me mad! Only do not leave me where I cannot find you! Oh, God! I cannot live without my life! I cannot live without my soul!

Catherine Earnshaw you shall not rest! You shall not rest!

INTERVAL

## Part Four

**Heathcliff** *appears like a ringmaster. He has a whip.*

**Heathcliff**
Are you still hungry?
Do you want more?
Do you want warmth and softness?
Forgiveness and resolve?

**The Moor**
Well what did you expect?
This man was found in loss,
Grown in hate
And hardened in revenge.
If you want Romance? Go to Cornwall.
If you want hope, look to the stars.
This is harsh harvest of hatred.
Well what did you expect?
Love?
There is no love here.

**The Moor** *welcomes* **Catherine** *into their number. They crown her with a bracken crown.*

**Catherine's Ghost** *and* **The Moor**
Love.
There is no love here.

**The Moor** *turns away.*

**Dr Kenneth** *wipes blood from his hands and packs up his things. He is like a clown at the circus.*

**Dr Kenneth**   Being a doctor, love is rather at the bottom of my list of priorities. I prefer to divert myself with things like life . . . and death. Of which there seems to be an increasing amount of these days. I used to be good at my job. Not the best, but I was adequate for a small Yorkshire town. But something's happened. Life seems to be slipping through my fingers at the moment. No sooner have I crossed the Moor to one sweaty deathbed, I'm called to another.

You'd think you'd get used to it – but now, they seem to be getting younger. Or am I getting older? I get confused. Frances Earnshaw, deceased. Catherine Linton, deceased. Hindley Earnshaw, deceased, and so many wretched others. And now I hear that poor Isabella Heathcliff has lost her grip, deceased. She lived a dozen years after leaving her husband and she brought up her child Little Linton with no help from Heathcliff – but she could hold on no longer. Her family are of a delicate constitution though. She and her brother, Edgar, both lack the ruddy health that is required in these parts. What her last illness was, I am not certain: a kind of fever, slow at its commencement, and rapidly consuming life towards the close. Totally incurable and there's nothing I could have done. Nothing! And why? Why do these things happen? Who decides who lives or dies?! What's the point of it all? What does it all mean?

I'm so sorry. I haven't got time for this, I've got to get to work, I best go and tell Mr Edgar the dreadful news about his sister. Soon he will not only have young Mistress Cathy, born of Catherine Linton, deceased, to take care of but also his nephew, Little Linton Heathcliff, son of Isabella Heathcliff, deceased. I fear Little Linton, son of Isabella Heathcliff, deceased, has his mother's weak disposition and I might not be able to tether him to this earth for long. At least in Miss Cathy, born of Catherine Linton, deceased, we have one from a good hardy stock. Let's hope that she lasts the course. Let's keep everything crossed.

*He crosses his fingers and legs.*

**Edgar** *appears.*

**Edgar**   Crossing one's fingers doesn't feel like the cutting edge of medical science, but I will happily join you if it is the best chance of receiving good tidings.

**Dr Kenneth**    I have news of your sister and nephew. Shall we go somewhere private?

**Edgar**    Oh Lord.

*They exit.* **Dr Kenneth** *still has his fingers crossed.*

**The Leader**    Death falls like a blanket of frost, but, like snowdrops in the February ground, fresh shoots push through.

**Young Cathy** *emerges from within their ranks.*

**Young Cathy**    My name's Cathy. Cathy Linton. What are we doing today?

**The Leader**    She was a miracle of a child. A wonder of warmth and curiosity but by the age of thirteen she had not once been beyond the range of her father's land by herself. Mr Linton would take her with him a mile or so outside; but he trusted her to no one else. Wuthering Heights and Mr Heathcliff did not exist for her: she was a perfect recluse . . .

**Young Cathy**    I want to go out! I want to go out!

**The Moor**    Ha!

**Young Cathy**    I wonder what lies on the other side? Is it the sea?

**The Leader**    No, Miss Cathy. It is hills again, just like these.

**Young Cathy**    And what are those golden rocks over there? And why are they bright so long after it is evening here?

**The Leader**    Because they are a great deal higher up than we are. In summer I have found snow under that black hollow on the north-east side!

**Young Cathy**    Can I go?

**Edgar** *appears. He seems sad and distracted.*

**Edgar**    They are not worth the trouble, my dear. Thrushcross Grange is the finest place in the world.

**Young Cathy** (*jumping on him*)    Papa! Let me go and find the summer snow! I know every inch and corner of Thrushcross Grange.

**Edgar**    Hush, hush.

**Young Cathy**    Papa! I want to see the frozen rock!

**Edgar**    Not now, love, not now. I have news.

**Young Cathy**    News?

**Edgar**    Your Aunt Isabella has died and your cousin, Linton needs us to give him a home. I am leaving for London to collect the poor boy. Do you understand?

**Young Cathy**    I understand, Papa, and will treat him as kindly as I would treat a puppy.

**Edgar**    Good girl.

**Young Cathy**    Papa?

**Edgar**    Yes?

**Young Cathy**    Whilst you are gone, might I venture out to the fairy cave?

**The Leader**    The road to the fairy cave wound close to Wuthering Heights.

**Edgar**    No. You may not. Not yet, love: not yet.

**Edgar** *puts on his coat and exits.*

**Young Cathy** *looks cheekily at* **The Moor** *and makes a run for it, slipping through their grasp like soap in bath.*

**The Moor**
    Ha!
    We shouldn't smile, but see how she
    strays from the path!
    Look as she slips from our grasp
    Like soap in a hot deep bath.
    Oi!

Watch it!
I said watch it wild one!
Ha!
We shouldn't laugh but this is
something we don't often see.
This is something rare and wild.
Like juniper and bog rosemary.

*They give chase and catch up with her far away from The Grange.*
*She throws off her cardigan with abandon and breathless joy.*

**Young Cathy**    Have you ever been to such a wild and
exciting place before?

**The Leader**    Stop this gallivanting and let's get ourselves
home.

**Young Cathy**    Make me!

**The Leader**    You are a cunning little fox.

**Young Cathy**    I am almost a woman!

**The Leader**    You are thirteen years old! You are a baby.

**Young Cathy**    Ever seen a baby run as fast as this?

**The Moor**
Ha!
We shouldn't smile, but see how she
strays from the path!
Look as she slips from our grasp
Like soap in a hot deep bath.

*She runs away and finds herself not only outside Wuthering*
*Heights, but also face to face with* **Hareton**. *Now eighteen, he is a*
*rough and fine-looking fellow.*

**The Leader**    Hareton Earnshaw. Last seen trying to rouse
the boozy corpse of his broken father. Look at him now!
Eighteen, angry and rough as the crags that surround him.

**Young Cathy**    Hello.

**Hareton**    Hello.

**Young Cathy**    Do you live here?

**Hareton**    I do.

**Young Cathy**    Is it your house?

**Hareton**    It is our house.

**Young Cathy**    Good. I am parched from all this running. If you invite me in, I might quench my thirst.

**Hareton**    Might you?

**Young Cathy**    Is this your father's house?

**Hareton**    Nay.

**Young Cathy**    Whose then?

**Hareton** *looks down.*

Are you a servant? Does this house belong to your master?

**The Leader**    Hold your tongue!

**Young Cathy**    I will not! When you said 'our house' I assumed you were the owner's son.

**The Leader**    Miss!

**Young Cathy**    Miss! You never called me 'Miss' which you should have done if you are a servant!

**The Leader**    Shhh!

**Hareton** *glares.*

**Young Cathy**    If you are a servant, get your horse. I want to see where the goblin-hunter rises in the marsh. What's the matter, boy? Get your horse, I say.

**Hareton**    I'll see thee damned before I'll be thy servant!

**Young Cathy**    How dare you speak to me like that?

**The Leader**    Softly! Softly! Mr Hareton is not a servant, he is not the master's son. Mr Hareton is your cousin.

**Young Cathy**    My cousin!

**The Leader**    Yes.

**Young Cathy**    My cousin is a gentleman's son. Papa has gone to fetch my cousin from London. To bring him home. This rude man is not my cousin!

**The Leader**    People can have many cousins without being any the worse for it.

**Edgar** *arrives back at Thrushcross Grange with* **Little Linton**. *He carries him in his arms, wrapped in a blanket.* **Little Linton** *whimpers.*

**Edgar**    Now, Cathy, your cousin is not as strong or as merry as you are.

Remember, he has just lost his mother, so don't expect him to play and run about with you immediately.

**Young Cathy** (*trying to see beneath the blanket*)    Hello Linton.

**Little Linton** (*pulling the blanket over his face*)    Go away!

**Edgar**    And don't harass him by talking too much. Let him be quiet this evening, at least, will you?

**Young Cathy**    Yes, yes, papa. But I do want to see his face. He hasn't looked out once.

**Edgar** *puts the sleeper down and releases the blanket.*

**Edgar**    Little Linton, this is your cousin Cathy. Cathy, this is your cousin Little Linton.

**Young Cathy** *smiles.* **Little Linton** *grimaces and whimpers.*

Don't cry, boy. Cathy is fond of you already and she doesn't want to hear you weeping.

**Young Cathy**    I do not.

**Little Linton** *gasps with grief.*

**Little Linton**   Let me go to bed, then.

**Young Cathy**   You cannot go to bed yet! We have so much to talk about.

*He begins to cry afresh.*

**Little Linton**   I can't sit on this chair. It is too hard.

**Young Cathy**   Go to the sofa, then.

**Little Linton** *slowly trails himself off, and lays down on a sofa.*
**Young Cathy** *pets her cousin, stroking his curls and kissing his cheek. She sings him to sleep.*

**Young Cathy**
  All hushed and still within the house,
  Without – all wind and driving rain;
  But something whispers in my mind,
  Through rain and through the wailing wind.

**Edgar**   I think he'll do very well here. The company of a child of his own age will instil new spirit into him. Yes. He'll do very well here.

*There is a loud knock at the door.* **Edgar** *opens the door to* **Hareton**.

**Hareton**   Heathcliff has sent me for his son.

**Edgar**   He is staying with us. Go away!

*He tries to close the door but* **Hareton**, *strong, stops it.*

**Hareton**   I said, Heathcliff has sent me for his son.

**Edgar**   Tell Mr Heathcliff that his son shall come to Wuthering Heights tomorrow. He is too tired to go the distance now.

**Hareton**   I will say it one more time, Heathcliff has sent me for his son!

**Hareton** *stands firm.*

*The cock crows.*

**Edgar**    Very well.

**The Leader**    You are letting him go?

**Edgar**    What else can I do? I have no influence over his destiny now, do I? Do I?

**The Leader**    You do not.

**Edgar**    Say nothing to Cathy. The last thing I want is for her to try to visit him at the Heights. I will tell her his father sent for him suddenly, and he has been obliged to leave us.

Take him. Now!

**Little Linton** *is very reluctant to be roused.*

**The Leader**    Wake up little whitebeam. You must go to your father and try to love him.

**Little Linton**    My father! Mamma never told me I had a father. Why didn't Mamma and he live together, as other people do? And why didn't Mamma speak to me about him?

**The Leader** (*carrying him to Wuthering Heights*)    Make haste!

**Little Linton**    Is she to go with us? The girl I saw yesterday?

**The Leader**    No.

**Little Linton**    Is Uncle?

**The Leader**    No.

**Little Linton**    Is my father as young, handsome and attentive as Uncle?

**The Leader**    He's as young, and handsome, but attentive is not a word I would use to describe Heathcliff.

**Little Linton**    I cannot fancy him then. I need to be surrounded by attentive people if I am to thrive.

**The Leader**    Really little White Admiral? Really?

**Little Linton**    Am I like my father?

**The Leader**    No. You are not like him at all.

**Little Linton** *is delivered to* **Heathcliff** *and Wuthering Heights by* **The Moor**. *He is deposited like a white chrysalis at* **Heathcliff**'s *feet.*

**Heathcliff**    Hello. I feared I should have to come down and fetch my property myself if you didn't arrive soon. Let me see.

**Heathcliff** *examines* **Little Linton**.

Gods! Have they reared it on snails and sour milk? It's worse than I expected!

**Little Linton** *runs back into the arms of* **The Moor** *and clings to them, but they push him away and back to his father.*

Come hither, son.

**Little Linton** *weeps.*

Tut, tut!

**Heathcliff** *stretches out a hand and drags him roughly between his knees, and then holds up his head by the chin.*

None of that nonsense! Thou art thy mother's child, Little Linton! Where is my share in thee, thou whimpering chicken?

*He takes off the boy's cap and pushes back his thick flaxen blond curls, feels his slender arms and his small fingers. During the examination* **Little Linton** *stops crying and lifts his great blue eyes to inspect the inspector.*

Do you know me?

**Little Linton**    No.

**Heathcliff**    You've heard of me, I daresay?

**Little Linton**    No.

**Heathcliff**    No? Your mother was a wicked slut to leave you in ignorance of the father you possessed.

**The Leader**   Be kind, Heathcliff. He's the only family you have.

**Heathcliff**   I'll be very kind to him! My son is the prospective owner of Thrushcross Grange, and I do not wish him to die until I am certain of inheriting the place. I'm bitterly disappointed with the whey-faced, whining wretch, but now that I own Wuthering Heights the thought of possessing The Grange is sufficient to make me endure him.

**Little Linton**   Don't leave me! I'll not stay here! I'll not stay here!

**Heathcliff** *closes the door and* **The Moor** *leaves the shouting child behind.*

*The wind rages and years pass.*

**The Moor**
   We're a bit confused,
   what's going on?
   What the bloody hell is happening?

**The Leader**   Three years just slipped by!

**The Moor**   Oh, you should have said.

**Young Cathy** *is now sixteen. She bashes the ground and a chaos of grouse fly around her in a panic.*

**Young Cathy**   I am sixteen now!

**The Leader**   Miss Cathy! What are you doing out here?

**Young Cathy**   I can roam where I please.

**The Leader** (*under her breath*)   As long as Mr Linton doesn't find out.

**Young Cathy**   What did you say?

**The Leader**   Nothing.

*She bashes the ground again and more grouse fly in a fluster.*
**Heathcliff** *and* **Hareton** *appear.*

**Heathcliff**    What are you doing? Plundering my nests?

**Young Cathy**    Papa told me there were hundreds up here, and I wished to see the eggs.

**Heathcliff**    And who is Papa?

**Young Cathy**    Mr Edgar Linton of Thrushcross Grange. And who are you?

**Heathcliff**    I am Heathcliff. And the owner of Wuthering Heights.

**Young Cathy** (*looking at* **Hareton**)    I've seen him before. Is he your son?

**Heathcliff**    No, this man is not my son, but I have a son, and you have seen him before too. Will you come into my house? You shall receive a kind welcome.

**Young Cathy** *goes towards the Heights but* **The Moor** *pulls* **Heathcliff** *back.*

**The Leader**    What's your plan, Heathcliff?

**Heathcliff**    My plan is that the two cousins will fall in love, and get married.

**The Leader**    But why?

**Heathcliff**    I am not content to own only Wuthering Heights. I will also be master of the Grange.

*He goes into the Heights where* **Young Cathy** *is face to face again with* **Little Linton**.

**Young Cathy**    What! Is that Little Linton?

**Heathcliff**    Yes, he is Little Linton. He is my son, your cousin and sixteen – just like you.

**Young Cathy** (*to* **Heathcliff**)    You are my uncle, then! I thought I liked you – though you were a little cross at first. Why don't you visit us at the Grange with Linton? To live all these years such close neighbours, and never see us, is odd!

**Heathcliff**   I visited it before you were born.

**Young Cathy** *throws her arms around* **Heathcliff** *and kisses him. He pushes her away.*

If you have any affection to spare, give it to Little Linton: it is wasted on me.

*She sits with* **Little Linton**.

You must not mention coming here to your Papa, unless you do not want to see your cousin again.

**Young Cathy**   Why? Did you and Papa quarrel?

**Heathcliff**   He thought me too poor to marry his sister and was shocked that I married her nonetheless: his pride was hurt, and he'll never forgive it.

**Young Cathy**   Well. If I may not come here, then Linton must come to The Grange!

**Little Linton**   Me? Come to the Grange? How?

**Young Cathy**   You can walk.

**Little Linton**   It will be too far for me.

**Young Cathy**   It's only four miles.

**Little Linton**   To walk four miles would kill me.

**Heathcliff** (*to* **The Moor**)   Oh, the frustrating vapid thing! He's so absorbed in drying his feet that he never looks at her . . . Little Linton!

**Little Linton**   Yes, father?

**Heathcliff** (*to* **Little Linton**)   Have you nothing to show your cousin? A rabbit or a weasel's nest? Take her into the garden, before you change your shoes.

**Little Linton** (*reluctant to move*)   Wouldn't you rather sit here?

**Young Cathy** (*casting a longing look to the door, eager to be active*) Maybe . . .

**Hareton** *takes off his shirt and washes himself.*

How is he my cousin?

**Heathcliff**   He is your mother's nephew. Ah! I see. You're the favourite among us, Hareton! You take her round the farm and mind you behave like a gentleman!

**Hareton** *and* **Young Cathy** *walk into the garden. He keeps his eyes low, she sneaks a peep at his handsome face.*

(*To the audience.*) I take pleasure in Hareton. Hareton is gold put to the use of paving-stones, whilst Linton is tin polished to imitate silver. If Hareton were born a fool I should not enjoy him so much. But he's no fool. And, having felt all the feelings he feels, I can sympathise with the creature. I know what he suffers and know that this is only the beginning of his suffering. I've broken him faster than his scoundrel of a father broken me. And brought him lower – for he takes a pride in his brutishness, pride in his disdain. I have taught him to scorn everything. I take pleasure in Hareton. But Little Linton. My own flesh and blood . . . Yields me nothing but loathing.

*He pulls* **Little Linton** *by his arm.*

Get up, you idle boy! Go after them!

**Little Linton** *gathers his energies, and leaves the hearth. He is slow so slow!* **Young Cathy** *looks at the inscription over the door. 'Believe in love and joy 1847'.*

**Young Cathy**   Look at that! Hareton, what is the meaning of the words over the door?

**Hareton**   I don't know. I cannot read it.

**Young Cathy**   What do you mean you can't read it?

**Little Linton** *joins them and giggles, the first show of humour he has exhibited.*

**Little Linton**   He does not know his letters! Could you believe in the existence of such a colossal dunce?

**Young Cathy**   Is there something the matter with him?

**Little Linton**   There's nothing the matter but laziness is there, Hareton Earnshaw?

**Hareton**   If you weren't more of a lass than a lad, I'd fell thee this minute!

**Little Linton**   Catherine, come. We can have a nice biscuit.

**Young Cathy** *helps* **Little Linton** *to run away from* **Hareton** *and she embraces him.*

**Young Cathy**   I will return. I promise I will be back tomorrow! And every day. My dear Linton.

*She leaves.*

*Back at The Grange.* **Edgar** *is clearly unwell.* **Dr Kenneth** *is examining him.*

**Young Cathy**   Papa! I really am extremely angry with you – only I'm also so pleased that I can't hide it! My cousin, Little Linton, is but a few miles away and you knew it.

Why did you deceive me? Is it because you disliked Mr Heathcliff? If so I . . .

**Edgar**   It is not because I disliked Mr Heathcliff, but because Mr Heathcliff is a most diabolical man, delighting to ruin those he hates.

**Dr Kenneth**   Try not to exert yourself sir.

**Young Cathy**   But Mr Heathcliff was quite cordial, Papa, and he didn't object to our seeing each other.

**Edgar**   No.

**Young Cathy**   Yes! He said I might come to his house when I pleased; only I must not tell you, because you had quarreled with him, and would not forgive him for marrying Aunt Isabella.

**Edgar**   No.

**Dr Kenneth**   Please, sir . . .

**Young Cathy**   You are the one to blame! Mr Heathcliff is willing to let Linton and I be friends and you are not.

**Edgar**   No!

**Dr Kenneth**   Sir!

**Edgar**   Heathcliff is to blame. Heathcliff is to blame for everything.

Isabella might have been living yet, if it had not been for him! Your mother might have been living yet if it were not for him!

**Young Cathy**   Papa!

**Dr Kenneth**   Mr Linton, your heart!

**Edgar**   Cathy. You may not visit Wuthering Heights or Mr Heathcliff again. Do you hear? I said do you hear?

**Young Cathy**   Yes Papa.

**Edgar**   Now return to your old amusements, and think no more of Linton or Heathcliff or the godforsaken dwelling that is Wuthering Heights.

**Edgar** *collapses and is tended to by* **Dr Kenneth**. **Young Cathy** *crumples and cries.*

**The Leader**   Why are you crying? Pity for yourself?

**Young Cathy**   I'm not crying for myself.

**The Leader**   Then for your father?

**Young Cathy**   I cry for Linton. He is expecting to see me tomorrow, and he'll be so disappointed. He'll wait for me, and I shan't come!

**The Leader**    He'll survive.

**Young Cathy**    He won't.

**The Leader**    You could write him a letter?

**Young Cathy**    I could!

**The Moor** *delivers letter after letter from* **Young Cathy** *to* **Little Linton**.

**Catherine's Ghost**
　　Paper love
　　Spins in the cooling breeze.

**Young Cathy**    I need paper.

**Catherine's Ghost**
　　Paper love
　　Runs in the rain.

**Young Cathy**    Bring me a quill.

**Catherine's Ghost**
　　Paper love lives
　　Like a butterfly,

**Young Cathy**    Send this to Linton.

**Catherine's Ghost**
　　Only to entertain.

　　Paper love sings for a few short breaths
　　Blows for a few sharp cheers.
　　It gasps and rattles for a few small deaths
　　And sobs with a tiny tear.

　　Paper love
　　Cannot stand the fire.
　　Paper love
　　Drowns in the flood
　　Paper love
　　Is a fool's desire.
　　For it's paper.
　　Not blood.

*The wind takes all the love letters into the air and they fly above the Moor.* **Heathcliff** *catches them, one by one, like a frog catching flies.*

**Heathcliff** (*calling across the Moor from Wuthering Heights*)
Ho, Miss Linton! Miss Linton!

**Young Cathy** (*calling back across the Moor*)    I mustn't speak to you, Mr Heathcliff. Papa says you are a wicked man. I will not speak with you.

**Heathcliff**    You will. I've got your letters, and if you show me any more attitude I'll send them directly to your father.

**Young Cathy**    No!

**Heathcliff**    Good. Then we understand each other. Linton is in love with you. He's dying for you; breaking his heart for you. He gets worse daily; and he'll be under the earth before summer, unless you restore him with your presence.

**Young Cathy**    Linton!

*She runs out of The Grange and leaps straight to* **Little Linton** *who she showers with tears and kisses.*

**Little Linton**    Is that you, Miss Linton? No! Don't kiss me, it takes my breath and I will not be able to get it back.

Will you shut the door, if you please? You left it open and it's so cold!

**Young Cathy**    If you're cold I'll stoke the fire . . .

**Little Linton**    No! I will be covered with ashes if you do that.

Why didn't you come before? You should have come, instead of writing. It tired me dreadfully reading those long letters.

**Young Cathy**    Linton? Are you glad to see me?

**Little Linton**    Yes, I am, Miss. But I have been upset that you did not come sooner, Miss.

**Young Cathy**    I wish you would say Cathy.

**Little Linton**    Catherine. Shall we, shall we have a little rest together? Resting is one of my favourite things to do.

*She strokes his soft hair.*

I don't like this pillow. It's not high enough.

**Young Cathy** *brings another.*

That's too high.

**Young Cathy**    How must I arrange it then?

*He wheedles up to her and puts his head on her lap.*

**Little Linton**    Like this. I will sit on it like a precious gem. We can be quite still and not talk. But you may sing a song. Begin.

**Young Cathy** *sings 'All Hushed and Still Within the House' by Emily Brontë.*

**Young Cathy**
  All hushed and still within the house
  Without – all wind and driving rain;
  But something whispers to my mind,
  Through rain and through wailing wind.

**All**
  Never again.
  Never again?
  Why not again?
  Memory has power as real as thine.

**Little Linton**    Never again? You must! Will you come again tomorrow?

**Young Cathy**    We'll see.

*They kiss.*

**Hareton** *interrupts them.*

**Hareton**    Miss Catherine! I can read the words, now.

**Young Cathy**    Wonderful! Let us hear you if you are grown so clever!

**Hareton**    Believe in love and joy.

**Young Cathy**    And the figures?

**Hareton**    I cannot tell them yet.

**Young Cathy**    You dunce!

**Little Linton**    Yes. Dunce, dunce, dunce, dunce, dunce!

**Young Cathy** *and* **Little Linton** *laugh and turn backs to* **Hareton**. **Hareton** *seizes* **Little Linton** *by the arm and swings him off his seat.*

**Hareton**    Get to your own room! And take her there if she comes to see you and you alone. Begone with you both! I don't want to watch your triflings!

**Little Linton** *starts to shriek.*

**Little Linton**    I'll kill you! Devil! Devil! I'll kill you! I'll kill you!

*He shrieks shockingly until his cries become choked by a fit of coughing; blood gushes from his mouth, and he falls to the ground.*

**Young Cathy**    Dr Kenneth! Please help me. Linton is dying. Please! Someone . . .

*We see* **Dr Kenneth** *running from the other side of* **The Moor** *but before he can get there,* **Hareton** *carries* **Little Linton** *to the sofa.* **Young Cathy** *tries to follow him.*

**Hareton**    Go home Miss Catherine. Go home. It is too bad here.

**Young Cathy**    You will not tell me what to do! I will tear the hair off my head if you do not let me see him! I will tell Papa what you did to him and you shall be put in prison and hanged!

**Hareton** (*tearful*)   Miss Catherine, I did not do this to him. He is sick. Please go home.

**Young Cathy** *pushes past the distraught* **Hareton**. **Little Linton** *is in a messy, sick, rage. He is being seen to by* **Dr Kenneth**.

**Young Cathy**   How is he, Doctor?

**Dr Kenneth**   Try not to worry.

**Little Linton**   Get away from me!

**Dr Kenneth** *goes to leave.*

Not you Doctor!

**Dr Kenneth** *returns to his side.*

You Catherine! You! You cause uproar and trouble.

**Young Cathy**   Me? It was him!

*She points to* **Hareton**.

**Little Linton**   It was not Hareton, it was you! I will not speak to you, I will not look at you, I will not abide you!

**Young Cathy**   Oh! If this is how you feel, I shall not stay. Goodbye.

**Heathcliff**   Tut tut.

**Heathcliff** *catches* **Little Linton**'*s eye sternly.*

**Little Linton**   Stay, Catherine. Please stay. I cannot help showing my nature to you. I regret it and repent it but it is because I love you!

**Young Cathy**   And I love you!

**Young Cathy** *and* **Little Linton** *embrace.*

**Edgar** *is in his deathbed at Thrushcross Grange.*

**Edgar**   Death. I've prayed often for the approach of what is coming, but now I begin to fear it. I thought the memory of the hour I came down that glen a bridegroom would be less sweet than the anticipation that I was soon to be carried up, and laid in its lonely hollow, with my Catherine!

But now I fear what I will leave behind. I cannot leave Cathy to a fate at Wuthering Heights. She has been a living hope by my side and I'd rather resign her to God, and lay her in the earth before me than see Heathcliff steal her light.

*He calls across the Moor.*

Come home! Cathy, come home!

**Dr Kenneth**    Miss Cathy, you must return.

**Young Cathy**    Linton, My father is very ill, I need to go to his bedside.

**Little Linton**    Don't leave me Catherine. I need you.

**Young Cathy**    I can't dance attendance on your affectations always. I don't only love you, I love my Papa. I need to go home.

**Dr Kenneth**    Miss Linton! Please.

**Little Linton**    Catherine!

*He grabs at her.*

**Young Cathy**    Get off me.

*He grabs her skirt.*

Rise, and don't degrade yourself into an abject reptile. Don't!

**Little Linton** *throws his nerveless frame along the ground. He seems convulsed with exquisite terror.*

**Little Linton**    I'm a traitor and I dare not tell you! But if you leave me, I shall be killed! Dear Catherine, my life is in your hands. Consent!

**Young Cathy**    Consent to what?

**Little Linton**   To stay. My father threatened me, and I dread him!

**Young Cathy**   I'm no coward. Save yourself for I am not afraid!

**Young Cathy** *goes to leave but* **Heathcliff** *blocks her way.*

**Heathcliff**   Get up, Little Linton!

**Young Cathy**   Mr Heathcliff.

**Heathcliff**   Miss Linton.

**Edgar** *calls across the Moor.*

**Edgar**   Cathy! Get away from Wuthering Heights!

**Heathcliff**   Get up, Linton! Don't grovel on the ground. Get up, this moment!

**Little Linton**   I will, Father. Catherine, give me your hand.

**Heathcliff**   No, stand on your own two feet.

**Little Linton** *stands.*

**Young Cathy**   I am leaving Wuthering Heights, Mr Heathcliff. Papa needs me. Linton, he'll not harm you, why are you so afraid?

**Little Linton**   You cannot leave.

**Heathcliff**   I am feeling hospitable today, Miss Linton. You must stay.

**Young Cathy**   I will not.

**Edgar**   Cathy!

**Young Cathy** *runs to the door but* **Heathcliff** *grabs her arm.*

**Heathcliff**   Sit down, and allow me to shut the door.

*He throws* **Young Cathy** *to the ground and locks the door.*

Miss Linton, I am not an ungenerous man. I am giving you the boy.

**Young Cathy** *glowers.*

How she does stare! What an unsettling urge I have to destroy anything that seems afraid of me!

*He draws in his breath, and strikes the table.*

By hell! I hate them.

**Young Cathy**    I am not afraid of you! Give me that key!

**Heathcliff**    Stand off, or I shall knock you down.

*She grabs his hand and tries to wrestle the key from him.*

**Young Cathy**    I will go!

**Heathcliff** *drops the key, she grabs it and he grabs her. He slaps her across the face over and over again.* **Young Cathy***, released, puts her hands to her temples, not sure whether her ears are off or on.* **Heathcliff** *picks up the key.*

**Heathcliff**    Go to Linton as I command, and cry at your ease! Tomorrow, when you and he are married, I shall be your second father. And, in a few short days when Edgar Linton meets his maker, I shall be your only father.

**Young Cathy**    No!

**Heathcliff**    And there is plenty more of this. (*He raises his hand.*) You shall have a daily taste if I catch such a temper in your eyes again! Naughty pet.

**Young Cathy** *weeps aloud.* **Little Linton** *shrinks into a corner, as quiet as a mouse, congratulating himself that the violence alighted on* **Young Cathy** *rather than him.* **Heathcliff** *leaves and* **Young Cathy** *immediately tries to escape. It is impossible.*

**Young Cathy**    Linton! What is your diabolical father after? What is your diabolical father after? Tell me, or I'll box your ears, as he has done mine.

**Little Linton** *smiles cruelly.*

It was for your sake I came. Tell me what he wants.

*He drinks his tea before speaking again. His anguish has subsided.*

**Little Linton**   Papa wants us to be married.

**Young Cathy**   Married?

**Little Linton**   Yes, Catherine. Married. He knows your Papa would forbid it and he's afraid I will die if we wait. If I die before we are married, you will inherit Thrushcross Grange. So we are to be married in the morning and you must stay here the night. If you do as he wishes, you shall return home next day, and take me with you.

**The Leader**   Pitiful changeling! Do you imagine that a healthy, hearty, shining girl like Cathy Linton would willingly tie herself to a little perishing stoat like you? You want whipping for trapping her with your dastardly tricks I shake you for your treachery, I shake you for your conceit!

**Little Linton**, *in alarm for his dear self again, clasps her in his two feeble arms, sobbing.*

**Little Linton**   You must obey my father and you must obey me. You must.

**Young Cathy**   I must obey my own. What will he think when I do not return home? I'll either break or burn a way out of the house. I love Papa better than you so don't test me!

**Heathcliff** *enters and holds the door open for* **Little Linton** *to slide through like a guilty spaniel. The lock is re-secured.*

**Young Cathy**   Mr Heathcliff, let me go home! I promise to marry Linton in good time.

**Heathcliff**   You shall not leave until it is done.

**Young Cathy**   Then marry us now and let me go home, for I must let Papa know I'm safe! He will fear I am lost.

**Heathcliff**   He'll fear you are tired of waiting on him and run off for a little amusement. His happiest days were over when your days began, Cathy.

He cursed you for coming into the world as did I, and he will curse you as he leaves. You remain a prisoner.

**Young Cathy**   If Papa dies before I return, how could I bear to live?

*She kneels.*

I'll not get up, and I'll not take my eyes from your face till you look back at me! Look! Have you never loved anybody in all your life? Never? Please. Look at me.

*She reaches to touch him.*

**Heathcliff**   Keep your fingers off me or I'll kick you! I'd rather be hugged by a snake! I will have my way.

*He shakes himself, as if his flesh crept with aversion, then backs her away until she can no longer be seen.*

**The Moor**   One day passes.

*We see **Little Linton** and **Young Cathy** married.*

Two days.

*We see them fighting.*

Three, four and five . . .

*We see **Young Cathy** locked in a room. We see **Little Linton**. He sucks a stick of sugar-candy.*

**The Leader**   Where is Miss Cathy?

*He sucks on his lolly like an innocent.*

Is she gone?

**Little Linton**   Gone? No! She's not to go. We won't let her. Papa says I'm not to be soft with Catherine. She's my wife now, and it's shameful that she should wish to leave me. Papa says she wants me to die so she can have my money, but she can't have it. She may cry, and she may be sick as much as she pleases but she never shall go home!

**The Moor**
  Be careful what you seed.
  This black bog will close its fist around
  anything it can snag.
  Cloudberry and Crowberry might dance
  on the surface –
  But the bullish bracken grips the bog in
  a headlock.

*At Thrushcross Grange* **Edgar** *is being tended to by* **Dr Kenneth**.

**Edgar**    Cathy . . . Cathy . . . Cathy . . .

**Young Cathy**    Papa . . . Papa . . . dear Papa . . .

**Little Linton**    She cries so much I can't bear it. Moaning and grieving all night long and so loud that I can't sleep.

**Heathcliff** *beckons* **Dr Kenneth** *away from* **Edgar** *and talks to him in earnest.* **Hareton** *listens at the door to* **Young Cathy**'s *room.*

**The Moor**
  A scatter of yellow stars might
  seem to welcome hope
  But the adder slides beneath
  The adder slides beneath.

**Edgar**    My darling girl, my darling poor girl.

**Little Linton**    I'm glad my uncle is dying, for I shall be master of the Grange when he is gone. Catherine always speaks of it as her house. But it isn't hers! It's mine!

**Heathcliff** *talks to lawyers and hands over money.*

**The Moor**
  And what of the rage that is planted?
  The hate and jealousy that has
  slipped into our watery beds?
  Oh they grow alright. They are
  coming along nicely, thank you.

**Young Cathy** *sits with her face to the wall.*

**Little Linton**   Papa says everything she has is mine. All her nice books are mine; she offered to give them to me if I would give her the key to our room and let her out. I told her she had nothing to give, they were all, all mine. And then she cried, and took a little locket from her neck, and said I should have that; two pictures in a gold case, on one side her mother, and on the other uncle, when they were young. I said they were mine, too; and tried to get them from her. The spiteful thing wouldn't let me: she pushed me off, and hurt me. I shrieked out and Papa came in. Papa asked what was the matter, and I explained. He ordered her to resign the pictures to me; she refused, and he struck her down, and wrenched it off the chain, and crushed it with his foot.

**The Moor**
   In the warm wet earth it grows.
   Be careful what you seed.

**Little Linton**   She's a naughty thing for crying continually; and she looks so pale and wild, I'm afraid of her.

*Unseen by* **Little Linton**, **Hareton** *releases* **Young Cathy** *from her room. She scrambles her way across the Moor to Thrushcross Grange and throws herself into* **Edgar**'s *arms. He dies blissfully kissing her cheek and murmuring.*

**Edgar**   Cathy!

**Young Cathy**   Papa, Papa! Papa!

**Edgar**   I am going to her. And you, darling child, shall come to us.

**Edgar** *reaches his hand to* **Catherine's Ghost**. *She lies beside him then slowly turns her back.*

*The mourners stand at the graveside.* **Young Cathy** *stands alone.* **Heathcliff** *arrives and* **Young Cathy** *tries to run away.*

**Heathcliff**   Stop! No more running away! I've come to fetch you home where you'll be a dutiful daughter. Linton's your concern now; I yield all my interest in him to you. He's such a cobweb, a pinch would annihilate him.

**Young Cathy**    I wish to stay at The Grange. Send Linton to me and I will look after him here.

**Heathcliff**    The Grange is mine now and I'm seeking a tenant. I want my children about me. Besides you owe me your services for your keep. I'm not going to nurture you in luxury and idleness after Linton is gone.

Come. Don't make me force you.

**Young Cathy**    I shall come. Linton is all I have to love in the world, and though you have done everything that you could to make him hateful to me, and me to him, you cannot make us hate each other.

**Heathcliff**    It is not I who will make him hateful to you, it is his own sweet spirit.

**Young Cathy**    Mr Heathcliff you have nobody to love you; and, however miserable you make us, we shall still have the revenge of knowing that your cruelty arises from your misery. You are lonely, like the devil.

Nobody loves you. Nobody will cry for you when you die! I wouldn't be you for the whole of the Moor!

**Heathcliff**    I am Nero. I am no ordinary man. I care deeply and care not at all.

**Young Cathy** *makes her way back to Wuthering Heights leaving* **Heathcliff** *at* **Edgar***'s grave.* **Catherine's Ghost***, lying beside him, looks up at* **Heathcliff** *and holds out her hand.*

**Heathcliff** *lies beside* **Catherine's Ghost***. They sing intimately, nose to nose as* **Edgar** *lies apart, silent and alone.*

**Catherine's Ghost**
    The Bluebell is the sweetest flower,
    That waves in summer air,
    Its blossoms have the mightiest power,
    To soothe my spirits care.

**Catherine's Ghost** *and* **Heathcliff**
The Bluebell cannot charm me now,
The heath has lost its bloom;
The violets in the glen below,
They yield no sweet perfume.

**The Leader**   Get out of that grave, Heathcliff! You must not disturb the dead!

**Heathcliff**   Me? Disturb her? She has disturbed me, night and day for eighteen years. Incessantly. Remorselessly. When I am dead . . .

**The Leader**   No, no Heathcliff!

**Heathcliff**   When I am dead, my body is to be carried to this grave. No minister need be called and no words be said over me.

**The Leader**   Leave the dead alone Heathcliff!

**Heathcliff**   I have struck loose one side of Catherine's coffin. When I'm laid there, one side of my coffin should be struck loose also. By the time Edgar gets to use in the afterlife, he'll not know which is which.

**The Leader**   No!

**Catherine's Ghost** *and* **Heathcliff** *embrace.* **The Moor** *breaks them up and leads* **Catherine's Ghost** *and* **Edgar** *away, leaving* **Heathcliff** *alone.*

**Young Cathy**   Doctor Kenneth! Doctor! Linton is gravely ill.

**Dr Kenneth** *comes running.*

**Heathcliff**   His life is not worth a farthing, and I won't spend a farthing on him.

**Dr Kenneth** *turns and runs away.*

**Young Cathy**   Doctor, please! If nobody will help me, he'll die!

**Heathcliff**    None here cares what becomes of him. If you care, act the nurse; if you do not, lock him up and leave him to die.

**The Moor**    One day passes.

*We see* **Little Linton** *close to death and* **Young Cathy** *nursing him.*

Two days.

*We see him fighting for life.*

Three, four and five . . .

**Little Linton** *dies. He leaves his body, picks up his candy and wanders across the Moor.*

*We see* **Young Cathy***, knees pulled up to her chest. She rings a bell . . .*

**Heathcliff**    How do you feel?

*She is silent.*

How do you feel, Catherine?

**Young Cathy**    Feel? I should feel glad to be alive. But I don't. You have left me alone for so long to struggle against death, that now I feel and see and smell only death.

**Heathcliff**    Good. You felt deeply and now you feel nothing. I smudge you.

**Heathcliff** *smiles. He walks away and sits on the Moor alone.*

**Epilogue**

*There is a huge gust of icy wind and Wuthering Heights as we saw it in the opening scene appears around them.*

**Lockwood** (*in a panic*)  What's happening? Where am I? Who am I?

**The Moor** *slaps him and he calms immediately.*

**The Leader**  You are Mr Lockwood, tenant of Thrushcross Grange. Time has passed and we are almost back where we started.

**Lockwood**  Thank you. Oh God. I remember now.

What became of Mr Heathcliff? I must make my peace with the troubled man.

**The Leader**  Heathcliff is dead. Three months since.

**Lockwood**  Dead? I am so, truly, truly sorry. How did it happen?

**The Leader**  One night, I heard him leave and he didn't return until morning. When he returned he looked different from his usual self.

**Lockwood**  Different? How?

**The Leader**  He was almost bright and cheerful. No, not cheerful – excited, and wild, and glad . . .

**Heathcliff**  Last night I was on the threshold of hell. Today, I am within sight of heaven. I am going to her.

Finally, finally, I will be with my Catherine again.

**The Leader**  You've been out all night. You have to rest.

**Heathcliff**  You might as well bid a man struggling in the water to rest when he is within reach of the shore! I have opened my eyes a hundred times a night to see her, only to be disappointed. But not anymore. Now I am with her again. I am pacified.

**Catherine's Ghost** *appears.*

There she is. Here is one who won't shrink from my company.

*He holds out his hand.*

By God! She is too much to bear.

**Heathcliff** *dies.*

**Catherine's Ghost** *takes* **Heathcliff**'*s hand and he rises. They rest foreheads together in deep peace before walking off together on the moors.*

**The Moor** (*softly*)
I am the Moor
My story was wide as the melting horizon
Deep as the roots that nurture.
My story was bigger than bitter revenges
Bigger than anger.
My story turned the planet.
And it's turning now.
But I let go . . .
I am the Moor

**Lockwood**    And what became of Young Cathy? My poor beneficent fairy.

**The Leader**    Why don't you knock on the door and find out?

**Lockwood** *looks reticent.*

Go on.

**Lockwood** *knocks at the door of Wuthering Heights.*

**Lockwood**    Hello. It is I. Lockwood.

**Hareton** *opens the door of Wuthering Heights. He is warm and friendly and wearing an apron. He wipes his hands as if he has been baking.*

**Hareton**    Mr Lockwood! Come in. Come in! (*Shouts.*) Cathy!

**Young Cathy** (*shouts*)   What is it?

**Young Cathy** *appears in the garden with a basket of flowers. She is in trousers and seems happy and free.*

**Hareton**   Mr Lockwood is paying us a visit.

**Young Cathy** *joins* **Hareton** *in the kitchen.*

**Young Cathy**   Welcome, Sir. It is good to see you again.

**Hareton**   Can I make you a cup of tea? I've got a Victoria sandwich in the oven as well, if we can tempt you to stay.

**Lockwood**   Tea? Victoria sandwich? Thank you, dear friends for this unexpectedly warm welcome. I would dearly love a cup of tea. But first, pray, tell me one thing.

**Young Cathy**   What would you like to know, Sir?

**Lockwood**   What gentle magic has happened here? How did you two souls come to look so happy? Please tell me how this wonder came to pass.

**Young Cathy**   It did not happen swiftly, sir. Our battered hearts took quite some time to heal.

**Hareton**   What she is trying to say, Sir, is that, after Heathcliff died, she was very cross with me.

**Young Cathy** (*laughing*)   And you with I, Hareton!

**The Moor** *crosses and we are back in time.*

**Young Cathy**, *sullen again, goes to get a book from the shelf but cannot reach.* **Hareton** *gets the book for her but she still sits separately and silently. He watches as she reads. He goes behind her and points at one of the pages. She pushes his hand away. Almost without thinking,* **Hareton** *reaches out and touches her hair, as gently as if it were a bird.*

**Young Cathy**   Get away this moment! How dare you touch me? I'll go upstairs again, if you come near me.

**Hareton** *retreats, but keeps watching the reading young woman. He turns to* **The Moor** *and talks to them out of a window.*

**Hareton**   Will you ask her to read to me? I'm tired of doing nothing; and I do like – I would like to hear her voice. Don't say I want it. Ask for yourself . . .

**The Moor** *knocks on the door and* **Young Cathy** *answers.*

**The Leader**   Hareton would like you to read to him, Cathy.

**Hareton**   I said don't say it was me!

**The Leader**   He'd be happy if you did him the kindness.

**Young Cathy**   I reject any pretence at friendship he has the hypocrisy to offer!

**The Moor**   She rejects any pretence at friendship you have the hypocrisy to offer.

**Hareton**   I heard her, thank you.

**Young Cathy** (*to* **Hareton**)   I despise you, and have nothing to say to you!

**Hareton**   I just wanted to . . .

**Young Cathy**   I would have given my life for one kind word, to see your face when Linton was sick, but no, you all kept off.

**Hareton**   What could I have done? How am I to blame?

**Young Cathy**   Be silent!

**Hareton**   But I tried! More than once . . .

**Young Cathy**   I'll go out of doors rather than have your disagreeable voice in my ear!

**Hareton**   Go to hell!

**Young Cathy** *and* **Hareton** *stubbornly turn their backs on each other.*

**The Moor**
  Home can come in many forms
  Person, place or beast
  It soothes the soul and strokes the brow
  Gives rest, for now, at least.

*Petals start to fall.*

**Hareton** *goes back to work.*

**Young Cathy**    Do you ever dream, Hareton? And, if you do, what do you dream about?

**Hareton** *is silent.*

Hareton, if I gave you a book now, would you take it?

**Hareton** *is silent.*

I shall try!

*She places one she had been perusing in his hand; he flings it away.*

**Hareton**    I'll break your neck if you do that again!

**Young Cathy**    Well, I shall put it here in case you change your mind.

*She places it on the floor.*

**The Leader**    He did not touch the book. His young eyes hid from certain pain. Her young eyes watched for certain pleasure.

**Young Cathy**    Hareton, I don't know what to do to make you talk to me.

*She stamps her foot.*

You shall take notice of me.

**Hareton**    I shall have nothing to do with you and your mucky pride! I'll go to hell before I look at you again!

**Young Cathy**    Hareton. Please. Be my companion.

**Hareton**    Companion! When you hate me?

**Young Cathy**   It is not I who hate you, it is you who hate me!

**Hareton**   You're a damned liar. I made him angry a hundred times by taking your part?

**Young Cathy**   I didn't know you took my part, and I was miserable and bitter at everybody; but now I thank you, and beg you to forgive me.

**The Moor**
Time can cool the heat of youth
Calm replaces rage
Silence now a scream drowns out.
Peace does war assuage.

Sun shines through the darkest clouds
Rainbow peeps through rain
Hate and fear all melt away
Hope and love remain.

**Young Cathy** *wraps her book neatly in white paper and ties it with a bit of ribbon. She leaves the gift on the floor.* **Hareton**, *softened, opens it and starts to read.* **Young Cathy** *sits beside him and gently helps him.* **Heathcliff**, **Catherine**, **Linton** *and* **The Moor** *gather to watch what is happening.*

**The Moor**   Look!

**Lockwood**   Something seems to have found its way in.

**The Moor**   What is it?

**The Leader**   It's love.

**The Moor**   Love?

**The Leader**   It must have bubbled up from a spring whilst we looked away.

**Lockwood**   Together, these fine young people will brave Satan and all his legions.

**Young Cathy** (*reading*)    And on New Year's Day, as they stepped through the door of Thrushcross Grange as wife and husband . . .

**Hareton**    They halted to take a last look at the moon.

*They all look up to the sky.*

**Young Cathy**    Or, more correctly, they took a last look at each other.

*They all look at each other.*

**Hareton**    Yes. They took a last, and first, look at each other by the light of the moon.

*They all look to the audience and sing quietly until night, peace and hope fall . . .*

**The Moor**    The End!

*The End.*

www.ingramcontent.com/pod-product-compliance
Ingram Content Group UK Ltd.
Pitfield, Milton Keynes, MK11 3LW, UK
UKHW020709280225
455688UK00012B/339